A Guide to Teaching Elementary Science

A Guide to Teaching Elementary Science

Ten Easy Steps

Yvette F. Greenspan

SENSE PUBLISHERS
ROTTERDAM/BOSTON/TAIPEI

A C.I.P. record for this book is available from the Library of Congress.

ISBN: 978-94-6300-365-0 (paperback)
ISBN: 978-94-6300-366-7 (hardback)
ISBN: 978-94-6300-367-4 (e-book)

Published by: Sense Publishers,
P.O. Box 21858,
3001 AW Rotterdam,
The Netherlands
https://www.sensepublishers.com/

All chapters in this book have undergone peer review.

Printed on acid-free paper

All Rights Reserved © 2016 Sense Publishers

No part of this work may be reproduced, stored in a retrieval system, or transmitted in any form or by any means, electronic, mechanical, photocopying, microfilming, recording or otherwise, without written permission from the Publisher, with the exception of any material supplied specifically for the purpose of being entered and executed on a computer system, for exclusive use by the purchaser of the work.

I dedicate this book to the many teachers I have known who have overcome tremendous obstacles to tirelessly inspire their students to love all that is science.

TABLE OF CONTENTS

PREFACE

PURPOSE OF THE TEXT

This book presents ten easy steps to help veteran, experienced, and novice teachers develop a sound, realistic, fun and exciting science curriculum within the guidelines of the Next Generation Science Standards and the Common Core Standards. It is:

- designed as a practical handbook for busy classroom teachers;
- organized to include best practices for teaching science;
- structured with easily implemented ideas and lesson plans that embrace and address the needs of *all* learners;
- prepared with extensive lists of resources.

The steps are designed with inquiry learning, thus engaging *all* students in the learning process through hands-on activities in cooperative learning groups. I wrote this book using everyday language and with simple descriptive examples that are thought-provoking and supported by leading researchers and verified by my extensive experience.

HOW TO BEST USE THIS GUIDEBOOK

Using this book will not consume large amounts of your time. As an elementary school teacher, I understand that your time is valuable and limited. That's why I designed this book to use before, during, or after you teach a science lesson or to peruse when it's convenient for you to reflect on the notion of how to teach science when your students are excited and motivated to learn.

ORGANIZATIONAL FEATURES OF THE TEXT

Part I

Rooted in the Next Generation Science Standards, the ten steps, basic and uncomplicated, are easily read and should prepare you to teach science through inquiry-based learning, the 5E Instructional Model, and the Scientific Method. Think about them in planning your science lessons and setting up effective science curricula. Take the ideas outlined and adapt them to the needs of your students and to your own needs as a teacher. Try them – they may not work effectively at first, but with time, you might find them helpful and worthwhile.

Part II

Part II of this book is devoted to sample lesson plans, which cover each of the areas of science required by the current standards. You will see lesson plans for both primary and intermediate grades in physical science, life science, earth and space, and engineering, technology and applications of science. Not only do they follow the 5E Instructional Model, a possible approach for teaching inquiry learning, emphasizing STEM, each lesson plan contains background information on the scientific concept, materials needed to teach each topic, the five phases for teaching the concept, possible home learning assignments, strategies to teach the Exceptional Student (ESE learners), some connections to other disciplines, and several real world applications. I have also included some of my favorite lesson plans. They, too, may be adapted, revised, and adjusted to meet the needs of your students. The unit on a place-based experience, a field trip, gives you science content in the disciplinary core ideas found in the Next Generation Science Standards and also integrates mathematics, social studies, and language arts' skills. The handouts are excellent teaching tools and can be adapted, too, for all grade levels.

Figures, Handouts and Appendices

The figures found throughout this guidebook and other handouts exhibited in the appendices should help you to incorporate the ten steps, always remembering that "nothing is written in stone;" the steps serve only as a source of information and a foundation to build on as you pursue new avenues of teaching. You'll find handouts for a science fair, including an elementary assessment, and other assessments I have used in my classroom and found to be most effective. Keep in mind that every handout can be adapted for your grade level and the ability of your students.

A Final Note

Take into consideration the ten steps outlined in this handbook. Add them as another source of information to help your students learn science. I believe they can only improve your teaching and your students' learning. As you embark on this new journey, or perhaps continue it, think of it as an exciting path toward greater understanding of all that is science.

ACKNOWLEDGEMENTS

Thank you to all the college professors, educators, administrators, mentors, and teachers who have inspired me to develop a passion for both learning and teaching science. I have learned from all of you.

Thanks also to my editor, Virginia McCullough, for her patience, expertise, and belief in my ability to complete this project. She has taken my words and made them vividly real so that they can benefit the educational community.

Thank you to Peter de Liefde and the staff at Sense Publishers for having confidence in me and for providing support and assistance in the editing, proofreading and design of this book.

Thank you to my family and friends who have encouraged me throughout this journey. You know who you are!

And, of course, I want to thank my husband and my children for their love, understanding, and constant reassurance during the many hours it took me to write this book and complete a lifelong goal.

Finally, to my grandchildren, who are learning that the world of science is all encompassing and plays an integral role in their everyday life: May you always be motivated and encouraged to observe, explore, learn, study, and research the true meaning of science.

LIST OF FIGURES AND TABLES

FIGURES

TABLES

INTRODUCTION

In a world filled with the products of scientific inquiry, scientific literacy has become a necessity for everyone. Everyone needs to use scientific information to make choices that arise every day. Everyone needs to be able to engage intelligently in public discourse and debate about important issues that involve science and technology. And everyone deserves to share in the excitement and personal fulfillment that can come from understanding and learning about the natural world.[1]

Teaching science should be fun and rewarding. Based on the premise that children have a natural curiosity about the things around them, teaching science would seem to be an easy task. Children wonder how plants grow and how animals live and move in their environment. They ask about how birds can fly and how high the sky stretches above them. They want to know why the moon glows and why it rains. So, given the nearly universal curiosity we see in children, why do some teachers have difficulty creating a classroom in which all students are engaged and enthusiastic about science learning? Based on my experience, many pre-service teachers and novice teachers, along with some veteran teachers, too, lack the know-how to create an active learning environment that promotes students' innate inquisitiveness, especially in culturally diverse classrooms.

In an effort to fill a gap in teaching tools, I created this practical, step-by-step handbook to provide guidelines to help you reach your goal of a successful science classroom for all learners. Regardless of experience level, pre-service or veteran, every reader will come away with a foundation of strategies that provide ideas to think about now and in the future.

Although I've designed the steps sequentially, you can adapt them to fit your teaching style, perhaps combining several steps or use them individually. I've also used the language, the 'jargon', of our profession. In addition, my purpose here is not to provide an abundance of details about every science classroom strategy. Rather, I chose to offer a brief course of action to heighten the awareness of science for both teachers and students. "After all, the ideal is to involve the students in their own learning while recognizing their prior experiences and encouraging them to be active learners."[2]

THE CURRENT STATE OF STUDENTS' SCIENCE PERFORMANCE

We see significant evidence indicating that when compared to children learning science in other countries around the world, students at various academic levels in the United States are not adequately learning basic science. The former president of the National Science Teachers Association (NSTA) remarked that learning science is an on-going process that begins in elementary school. She states:

> ...teachers are often surprised to find middle school and high school students have major misconceptions about fundamental ideas developed early on that went unchallenged through school. They are also dismayed to find there are often large gaps in students' conceptual understanding for even basic ideas in science . Is it reasonable for a school district to eliminate science for six years and then expect students to fill in the blanks in middle and high school? Science learning is a cumulative process.[3]

What about the state of science education at the college level? According to a 2014 article in *The New York Times*, Pérez-Peña concludes that students do better with a more active approach to learning science. He notes that after science educators overhauled the teaching strategies of an introductory physics class at the University of Colorado, students' scores improved approximately fifty percent more than those classes taught in traditional fashion. Similar results were found at the University of North Carolina in introductory biology classes. Further, the new strategies proved more beneficial for black students and those whose parents did not go to college.

Given these findings, it seems evident that our colleges should reinvent the way they teach science. However, generally speaking, this isn't the trend. Some explanations reveal that many tenured professors prefer to teach by lecturing and do not like to change what they believe works for them. Therefore, they find it difficult to create a classroom that is more student-oriented, one in which students work in teams and that incorporates new technologies. Pérez-Peña says, "At four-year colleges, 28 percent of students set out as math, engineering and science majors, but only 16 percent of bachelor's degrees are awarded in those fields."[4] Perhaps it's time to rethink how we teach science at the college level.

ASSESSING SCIENCE ACHIEVEMENT

One of the ways we examine science achievement is through assessments administered nationally and internationally. The "Trends in International Mathematics and Science Study (TIMSS)" is a series of international assessments of the mathematics and science achievement of students around the world. Since 1995, the assessment has been given internationally to fourth and eighth-graders every four years. The TIMSS suggests that when compared to students in other countries, fourth graders in the U.S. have shown no significant detectable change in science achievement during that timeframe.[5] For eighth graders, the trend appears more positive but our U.S. students' scores still lag behind the front running Asian countries.[6]

What do these results say about our science teaching at these grade levels? We have to ask ourselves if as teachers we're preparing our students to meet the demands of competing in the twenty-first century technological world. Are we addressing all of the needs of our minority students, who currently comprise 36% of our population, but make up more than half of all children born in the U.S. today?[7]

THE ACHIEVEMENT GAP

Why do we continue to see these disappointing test results? Although it is difficult to pinpoint one particular reason, a science achievement gap still exists among minority students and others students from diverse cultural backgrounds. According to the No Child Left Behind Act of 2001, *all* students were required to achieve high academic standards in core subject areas. However, although recent outcomes indicate that test scores have improved, a gap remains between white students and African American and Hispanic students, especially in the upper grades.[8]

Furthermore, Fensterwald concludes that the gap starts early in elementary school, widens in middle school, and continues, through filters and barriers, on a trajectory of low achievement and missed opportunities for minority groups. He claims that by the end of college, the number of Latinos and African Americans who graduate with degrees in science, technology, engineering, and mathematics is a trickle of the population.[9]

In addition, we see a relatively stable science achievement gap in the way Hispanic students perform as compared to white students, with white students outperforming Hispanic students. Researchers explain that teachers appear to be unprepared to meet the learning needs of English-language learners[10] because they have not received significant professional training in cultural differences. According to Bryan and Atwater:

> If teacher education programs do not assist science teachers in uncovering and critiquing their beliefs about students and teaching, we will continue to have teachers who rely on their cultural models that contain negative stereotypes (beliefs) and prejudices (attitudes) about culturally diverse students, their parents, and communities. "Science for all" will not become a reality for all U.S. students.[11]

Others agree that teachers who are inadequately prepared to teach science or use its teaching strategies[12] are faced with a growing number of English Language Learners (ELL) in their classrooms. These students "frequently confront the demands of academic learning through a yet-unmastered language without the instructional support they need."[13] Therefore, in order to improve the science literacy of their ELL students, teachers need professional development intervention to "improve their knowledge and practices in teaching science while promoting English language development of ELL students in urban schools."[14]

Moreover, according to Parsons, African American students, the second largest minority group in the United States, perform poorly in science achievement in the early grades, a trend that becomes more pronounced as they reach high school. Based on her findings, she found that culturally congruent instruction and the context in which African Americans learned science affected their success in that subject. In her article, she analyzes the cross-cultural work of Au and Kawakami, who connect culture, context, and learning by incorporating the ethnic minorities' culture into the education process. She contends that teaching content to these students should contain relevant cultural examples along with meaningful strategies.[15]

Others agree that we see a declining number of African American students in mathematics and science, particularly in STEM related fields. The reasons for this decline include perception of those subjects, lack of mentoring, stereotyping, and economic shortfalls.[16] On a more positive note, however, in recent years dropout rates have fallen steeply for all minority groups, including African American, Hispanic, and low-income young people; college attendance among the same groups has jumped sharply. Still, in 2014, students from low-income families complete college at only one-seventh the rate of those from high-income families.[17]

Not only are African American students and Hispanics not achieving the kind of success needed to understand basic science concepts, but girls also fall into this category. Patrick, Mantzicopoulos, and Samarapungavan noted that according to the United States Department of Education, girls are underrepresented in degrees earned and careers related to physical science, computer and information science, and engineering. Because girls are less likely to study science-oriented subjects and don't select non-compulsory science classes in high school, they have minimized their opportunity to access high-paying careers.[18] Furthermore, St. Rose states, "it is true that women are underrepresented in high-paying jobs, like those in science, technology, engineering and mathematics (STEM) fields. But it's not that simple as women not choosing STEM – they're often actively discouraged from pursuing careers in those fields."[19]

What, then, discourages girls? What influences girls' motivation (or the lack of it) to learn science? In a research study conducted in a large urban community, elementary school girls in third and fifth grade were observed learning science in a classroom setting with boys and other girls. Observers noted that cultural and societal factors had an appreciable effect on how girls appeared to have learned science. The qualitative study included observations, interviews, and a questionnaire; the results mirrored previous studies, which indicated that girls are generally conscious about their interrelationships with boys; this then affects their self-perception and the way others perceive them. As a consequence, girls modify their behavior and alter the way they learn science.[20] This is certainly a possible influence that discourages girls to choose science related careers.

A CALL FOR ACTION

Given the performance among all students in the U.S. and the gap among certain groups of students, I call upon you to act now and cultivate a love for all things science. It's within your power to help your students improve their knowledge of science, enrich the process of understanding science, develop their ability to think critically, and facilitate their proficiency in connecting and applying science concepts to everyday life . As professionals, it's our responsibility to enhance science learning for every student, whatever their race, culture, or gender. We are called on to foster students' natural curiosity so that they can reach their full potential and acquire the necessary science skills to live productively in the twenty-first century. Without a doubt, children from all backgrounds are capable of being successful in science.[21]

This ten-step handbook is designed as a tool to help you expand your views on science education and develop curricula that include the process of inquiry-based science. These ten steps will help you create a learning environment that emphasizes hands-on discovery and exploration of scientific concepts. Consider this a guide, which when implemented should help you create a classroom setting that is fun and engaging for all your students . Follow these ten easy steps I've outlined and you and your students can grow together toward understanding your scientific world.

NOTES

[1] National Committee on Science Education Standards and National Research Council. (1996). *National science education standards* (p. 1). Retrieved from http://www.nap.edu/openbook.php?record_id=4962&page=1

[2] Gilmer, P. J. (1999). *Looking at science as a pattern: Learning from differing perspectives* (p. 4). Presented at the annual meeting, National Association for Research in Science Teaching. Boston, MA.

[3] Keeley, P. (2009, May). Elementary science education in the K-12 System. *NSTA Reports, 20*, 3.

[4] Pérez-Peña, R. (2014, December 26). Colleges reinvent classes to keep more students in science. *The New York Times* (p. 2). Retrieved from http://www.nytimes.com/2014/12/27/us/college-science-classes-failure-rates-soar-go-back-to-drawing-board.html

[5] Gonzales, P., Williams T., Jocelyn, L., Roey, S., Kastberg, D., & Brenwald, S. (2008, December 9). *Highlights from TIMSS 2007: Mathematics and science achievement of U.S. fourth- and eighth-grade students in an international context.* Washington, DC: National Center for Education Statistics, Institute of Education Sciences, U.S. Department of Education. Retrieved from http://nces.ed.gov/timss/results11.asp

[6] National Center for Education Statistics. (2011). *Trends in international mathematics and science study (TIMSS).* Retrieved from http://nces.ed.gov/timss/results11_science11.asp

[7] Act for Youth: Center for Excellence. (2015). *U.S. teen demographics.* Retrieved from http://www.actforyouth.net/adolescence/demographics

[8] Bohrnstedt, G. (2013, October 30). *Gains and gaps: Education performance after a nation at risk.* Retrieved from http://www.air.org/resource/three-decades-education-reform-are-we-still-nation-risk

[9] Fensterwald, J. (2012). *STEMing the minority gap.* Retrieved from http://toped.svefoundation.org/2012/04/03/steming-the-minority-gap/

[10] Truby, R. (1998). *Student work and teacher practices in science* (NCES#1999-455). Washington, DC: National Center for Education Statistics.

[11] Bryan, L., & Atwater, M. (2002). Teacher beliefs and cultural models: A challenge for science teacher preparation programs. *Science Education, 86*, 826.

[12] Kennedy, M. (1998). *Form and substance in in-service teacher education* (Research Monograph No. 13). Madison, WI: University of Wisconsin, National Institute for Science Education.

[13] Lee, O., Maerten-Rivera, J., Penfield, R. D., LeRoy, K., & Secada, W. G. (2008, January). Science achievement of English language learners in urban elementary schools: Results of a first-year professional development intervention. *Journal of Research in Science Teaching, 45,* 32.

[14] Lee, O., Maerten-Rivera, J., Penfield, R. D., LeRoy, K., & Secada, W. G. (2008, January). Science achievement of English language learners in urban elementary schools: Results of a first-year professional development intervention. *Journal of Research in Science Teaching, 45,* 32.

[15] Parsons, E. C. (2008, August). Learning contexts, Black cultural ethos, and the science achievement of African American students in an urban middle school. *Journal of Research in Science Teaching, 45,* 665–683.

[16] National Center for Education Statistics. (2011). *Fast facts: Degrees conferred by race and sex.* Retrieved from http://nces.ed.gov/FastFacts/display.asp?id=72

[17] National Center for Education Statistics. (2014). *Progress for American children.* Retrieved from http://www.ed.gov/priorities

[18] Patrick, H., Mantzicopoulos, P., & Samarapungavan, A. (2009, February). Motivation for learning science in kindergarten: Is there a gender gap and does integrated inquiry and literacy instruction make a difference? *Journal of Research in Science Teaching, 46,* 166–191.

[19] St. Rose, A. (2013, Winter). Community college: Training ground for women in STEM? *Outlook, 107,* 20–21.

[20] Greenspan, Y. F. (2000). *Gender differences in an elementary school learning environment : A study on how girls learn science in collaborative learning groups.* Ann Arbor, MI: Bell & Howell Information and Learning Company.

[21] Duschl, R. A., Schweingruber, H. A., & Shouse, A. W. (2007). *Taking science to school: Learning and teaching science in grades K-8.* Washington, DC: The National Academies Press.

PART I

TEN EASY STEPS

STEP ONE

Know What You Want to Accomplish

The important thing in science is not so much to obtain new facts as to discover new ways of thinking about them.

William Lawrence Bragg

Science is complex to teach, in no small part because it's always changing. Your first priority is understanding the content you're about to teach. (If you are not familiar with the science concept at hand, use the resources mentioned below.) However, it's fine to learn along with your students, and they'll admire you for living the reality that scientific knowledge is expanding rapidly. After all, the ideal classroom is one in which the students and teacher grow and evolve into a community of learners.[1]

Ask yourself what you want to learn about the concept, what content is required, and your students' current level of understanding of the topic. As you develop your students' curiosity, try to widen yours. If possible, read books and magazines on the topic, research current practices, use students' textbooks or your Teacher's Guide as a reference, discuss the topic with colleagues, browse the Internet, and attend professional development workshops. All of these will help you prepare for what you want to accomplish.

ORGANIZE AND PLAN

Organizing and planning your lessons are the most important and time-consuming tasks involved in teaching, whether the subject is language arts, mathematics, social studies, or science. However, gathering the tools and planning lessons to meet your objectives are necessary steps to ensure success. (Check out suggestions for inquiry learning and the lesson plan format for the 5-E Instructional Model detailed in Step Five).

PLANNING A SCIENCE CURRICULUM

The groundwork for all science lesson planning is derived from the National Science Education Standards, published in 1996. "Standards are not a curriculum. They are not a set of lesson plans. They are goals for achievement that are appropriate for all members of the science education community."[2] Most recently, the Next Generation Science Standards were released; their goal is to better prepare students to think

3

critically, engage them in more relevant context, and apply science to their daily lives.[3] The Standards are divided into three main areas:

1. *Performance expectations*: Performances that can be assessed to determine if students meet the standards on what they should know and understand.
2. *Disciplinary Core Ideas*: Each performance expectation incorporates disciplinary core ideas (physical science, life science, earth and space, engineering, technology and applications of science), cross-cutting concepts (patterns, cause and effect, systems, energy, structure, and stability), and a science and engineering practice.
3. *Connections to other ideas and Common Core*: Each set of performance expectations lists connections to other ideas within science and engineering, and with the Common Core State Standards (see below) in mathematics and language arts.[4,5]

By following the guidelines set forth in these Standards, teachers know what they need to accomplish in their science classrooms.

In addition, statewide standards, those known as Common Core Standards,[6] were developed by a team of educators that included teachers, administrators, and national organizations. Their mission was to upgrade state standards by adopting a common core of internationally benchmarked standards in mathematics and language arts for grades K-12. The objective of the Common Core Standards is to ensure that students of that state become equipped with the necessary knowledge and skills in mathematics and language arts to be competitive globally. Although the Common Core Standards are not yet written for science, expectations are that science content would be integrated into the teaching of both mathematics and language arts.

Next, consider how you'll plan your lessons. Develop a unit of study, a series of easy-flowing and sequentially-targeted lessons, which correlate with the Next Generation Science Standards and the Common Core Standards mentioned above. Both the National Research Council[7] and the Institute for Inquiry[8] recommend that the goals or outcomes for most science lessons should focus on teaching both science content and the science process skills (now referred to as Practices in the Next Generation Science Standards): observing, measuring, inferring, classifying, predicting, and communicating (see Step Seven). Plan ahead, always remembering that your planning depends on the cognitive and maturation levels of your students. Consider a format for lesson development, incorporating inquiry-based learning, which includes the five phases[9] of engagement, exploration, explanation, elaboration, evaluation (discussed in Step Five).

By the same token, try to organize your investigations/experiments during your planning periods, a time when students aren't present. Further, prepare well in advance with all materials you need to conduct the investigation. Good preparation decreases stress and promotes a safe learning environment that ensures maximum learning. At the time you present the lesson itself, your materials should be ready to distribute to your students. Your preparation then gives you ample time to interact with your students and guide them through the learning process.

THE NEED TO BE FLEXIBLE

Finally, try to be flexible. Think about all the issues that could affect your curriculum, from planning your lessons, gathering your manipulatives, and/or organizing your experiments. You may need to be flexible in any number of areas to accommodate your students' needs. Students' classroom behavior and their readiness to learn, potential parent requests, and possible administration directives might call on you to modify your lesson plan as you teach. When time is short, you may need to change your plan and complete the topic at another time or make changes to teach it in the next hour or the next day.

In addition, be flexible if the manipulatives you need to conduct an experiment aren't immediately available – they could be hidden in closets, cabinets, or boxes in other classrooms in the school (see Step Six). If you need to, tap into the resources at your school; ask administrators, other teachers, or even your students if they know where the materials are located.

If the tools you need for conducting a particular lesson are unavailable, solicit donations from local businesses or check the catalogues of various scientific companies, such as:

- Carolina Biological Supply   www.carolina.com
- ETA Hand2Mind   www.hand2mind.com
- Frey Scientific   www.freyscientific.com
- Explore Learning   www.explorelearning.com
- Pasco Scientific   www.pasco.com

Of course, request monetary help from your administrator before purchasing the manipulatives, or ask your students' parents to donate the materials (see Step Six). You'll experience much less frustration if you take steps to acquire the materials your students need for their experiments.

KEY POINTS

- Know what you want to accomplish in your science curriculum.
- Find out what you need to learn in order to teach a specific scientific concept.
- Develop a curriculum aligned to the Next Generation Science Standards or the Common Core Standards.
- Create lesson plans that include inquiry-based learning, and, most importantly, be flexible during your planning time and in your teaching.

NOTES

[1] Tobin, K., & Tippins, D. (1993). Constructivism as a referent for teaching and learning. In K. Tobin (Ed.), *The practice of constructivism in science education* (pp. 3–21). Hillsdale, NJ: Lawrence Erlbaum Associates.

2 Kendall Hunt Publishing Company. (2014). *National science education standards* (p. 1). Retrieved from http://www.mykhscience.com/standards.html

3 National Science Teachers Association. (2009). *National science education standards*. Retrieved from http://www.nsta.org/publications/nses.aspx

4 Next Generation Science Standards. (2013, May). *Appendix M: Connections to the common core state standards for literacy in science and technical subjects.* Retrieved from http://www.nextgenscience.org/sites/ngss/files/Appendix%20M%20Connections%20to%20the%20CCSS%20for%20Literacy_061213.pdf

5 Committee on Development of an Addendum to the National Science Education Standards on Scientific Inquiry, Center for Science, Mathematics and Engineering Education & National research Council. (2000). *Inquiry and the national science education standards: A guide for teaching and learning.* Washington, DC: National Academy Press.

6 Common Core Standards. (2015). *Preparing America's students for success.* Retrieved from http://www.corestandards.org/

7 National Research Council. (1996). *National science education standards.* Retrieved from http://serc.carleton.edu/resources/1572.html

8 Exploratorium Institute for Inquiry. (2006). *Assessing for learning: Workshops designed to introduce teachers to formative assessment* (Workshops I–IV). San Francisco, CA. Retrieved from www.exploratorium.edu/ifi/workshops/assessing

9 *BSCS 5E Instructional Model.* (2012). Retrieved from http://www.bscs.org/bscs-5e-instructional-model

STEP TWO

Set the Stage

Imagination is more important than knowledge.
Albert Einstein

Setting the stage or creating an atmosphere that promotes a love of learning is as important as planning a viable science curriculum. Being familiar with each of your students helps you become aware of the many factors that affect how they learn in the classroom. In addition, when teachers present a scientific concept, they must address misconceptions students already have about the topic. As Bransford, Brown and Cocking note, "Before students can really learn new scientific concepts, they often need to re-conceptualize deeply rooted misconceptions that interfere with the learning."[1]

In other words, as we experience and observe the physical world, we construct a view that we stubbornly stick to whether or not it conflicts with scientific concepts. One example would be the way we think about a leaf and rock falling to the ground. Most of us reason that the rock falls faster than a leaf because it is heavier and the leaf is lighter. As we think about Newton's apple falling from the tree, we now know that a heavier object does not always fall to the ground more quickly than a lighter object because when dropped from the same height, objects fall to the earth at the same time when no major amount of air mass is acting upon them. Once we actually perform the task, we realize that our understanding is incorrect and we are forced to accept a new view.

THE CONSTRUCTIVIST LEARNING THEORY

Using the Constructivist Learning Theory as a guide, we can assume that individuals build knowledge based on previous experiences, constructed by making sense of these personal experiences in a social context.[2-4] In other words, learners construct their own knowledge and develop meaning based on that knowledge. That's why a pre-knowledge phase gives the teacher an awareness of what the student knows at the onset. Let's think about the impact of a heavier moving truck colliding with a small car. Most know, based on their experiences, that the truck will do much more damage to the car just because it is bigger and, therefore, in their thinking, can exert a larger force. However, Newton's Law states that two interacting bodies exert equal and opposite forces on each other. Therefore, students should be given opportunities to explore such misconceptions together to change their initial construct and cultivate a new one.

In the final analysis, this pre-teaching phase allows the teacher to understand what drives a student to understand a science concept. The teacher can then correct students' ideas and guide them toward a better comprehension of the goals of the lesson and, at the same time, students can take on the responsibility to move forward and learn the concept.

TEACHER EFFICACY

Let's consider the student/teacher roles. The student is expected to cooperate, become an active learner, and complete the task. However, what should we expect from teachers in a student-oriented learning environment? According to Ashton[5] there are two components to teacher expectations:

- the teacher believes that students, generally speaking, can learn the material.
- the teacher believes that some of these students can learn under his or her direction.

Ashton further reports there are eight dimensions to the development of teacher efficacy:

1. A sense of personal accomplishment	The teacher must view the work as meaningful and important.
2. Positive expectations for student behavior and achievement	The teacher must expect students to progress.
3. Personal responsibility for student learning	Accepts accountability and shows a willingness to examine performance.
4. Strategies for achieving objectives	Must plan for student learning, set goals for themselves, and identify strategies to achieve them.
5. Positive affect	Feels good about teaching, about self, and about students.
6. Sense of control	Believes (s)he can influence student learning.
7. Sense of common teacher/student goals	Develops a joint venture with students to accomplish goals.
8. Democratic decision making	Involves students in making decisions regarding goals and strategies.

Figure 1. Dimensions of teacher efficacy. The eight dimensions suggest that teacher effectiveness is rooted in a positive attitude toward their own abilities and their responsibilities and goals, paired with student cooperation[6]

Based on Ashton's beliefs about teacher effectiveness and expectations, the notion evolves that students take responsibility for their own learning while teachers provide the necessary manipulatives and tools with which to discover and learn. In other words, the teacher, as a guide, establishes a community of learners that expects students to engage with each other and ultimately succeed in learning science.

QUESTIONING TECHNIQUES

The manner in which teachers approach questioning students is key in determining if a student understands a concept or simply recalls information. This is the reason questioning strategies should be open-ended and provoke thought, enhance critical thinking, and give the teacher access to how students think. Once you know their ideas, you can encourage students to test them. The way a teacher forms a question and then responds to an answer also determines if the students are comfortable enough to openly express themselves.

Manktelow and Carlson[7] define questions as either closed or open. A closed question requires a simple response of yes or no, or it might be answered with a short response. A closed question tests students' understanding or concludes a discussion; these kinds of questions also can stop a conversation and create long silences. On the other hand, an open question requires the student to think about the response. These questions usually begin with what, why or how, but they could also start with a phrase or word that implies expansiveness, such as "tell me," or "describe." An open question elicits students' knowledge, opinions, or feelings and encourages them to provide details and further explore other issues.

According to Exploratorium[8] we can identify four categories of questioning in inquiry learning:

- Subject-centered, in which only one correct answer is possible.
- Person-centered, in which no wrong or right answer exists because the question asks what the student thinks.
- Process-centered, in which students must do something, using process skills, such as observing, measuring, inferring, and classifying.
- Other skills that do not fit into any of the above categories.

Obviously, an inquiry-based learning environment should emphasize more person-centered and process-centered questions.

Keep in mind that questions provide more than information about what students are learning. Open questions also help:

- build a bond between teachers and students;
- both teachers and students reflect on the topic;
- guide students through their misconceptions and eliminate them; and
- encourage students to embrace new ideas.

Ask open-ended questions in both small group discussions or with the whole classroom group, and in either case, use visual graphic organizers (see Step Four) to begin a dialogue. Or, use questions to start a brainstorming session on a specific topic such as push/pull, living/nonliving, sink/float, evaporation/condensation, and so forth.

Equally important to asking the right kind of question is the manner in which a teacher responds to a student's answer. For example, if you respond by saying, "any questions" or "is that clear?" or "okay?" you're inadvertently telling your students that they shouldn't have any questions and deadens further discussion. Better to say, "I bet you have some questions now – maybe I can answer them!" This implies that you're interested in what they have to say.

When addressing questions, first focus on the entire class rather than the individual student so that the student is not singled out. Next, be positive, direct, loving, constructive, encouraging, and helpful. If the question is a good one, tell the student as much; if the response is off task or inconsequential to the topic, respond with a different kind of statement, such as: "That's very interesting," "I like what you're saying," or "Let's talk about that later." Finally, if you're unsure about a response or simply want to involve your students in the process, throw the question back to them.[9]

DEVELOP A SCIENCE DISCOURSE

Many researchers have studied the importance of teachers and students discussing scientific concepts together, either in a whole class setting or in small groups. For example, Gallas[10] describes the way implementing "talking science" can transform the way we teach science and over time, changes the teacher's role. She views classroom science as a place for discourse, with its own language and thinking practices and describes the outcome for students in this child-centered approach. In other words, when students discuss the language of science throughout the learning process, it enhances their understandings of scientific concepts and provokes further thought.

ENHANCE STUDENTS' NATURAL CURIOSITY

Along these same lines, you can set the stage by enhancing your students' natural curiosity; they already have an innate desire to learn about the world first-hand, which is why it's important to provide ample and meaningful opportunities to develop a love of learning science. Their eagerness to explore and discover is inherent, but as they observe and experience the world, they may develop misconceptions. For example, based on observation alone, they may conclude the sun rises in the morning at the same place, or the same stars appear in the sky every night, seasons are caused by the distance between the earth and the sun, the moon can only been seen at night, mass and weight are the same, and rocks must be heavy.[11]

Teachers should provide many hands-on activities so students can work through their misconceptions, change their beliefs, and reconceptualize their views. As they face these challenges and learn to solve problems effortlessly, students can apply the process to real-world situations.

KEY POINTS

- Guide students through their misconceptions as you encourage their curiosity about the world around them.
- Be mindful of the environment – the atmosphere – you create in your classroom.
- Stimulate science discourse through open questions and the manner in which you respond to their answers.
- Inspire your students to love science by using their inherent curiosity about the world.

NOTES

[1] Bransford, J. D., Brown, A. L., & Cocking, R. R. (Eds.). (1999). *How people learn: Brain, mind, experience, and school* (p. 167). Washington, DC: National Academy Press.

[2] Driver, R., Squires, A., Rushworth, P., & Wood-Robinson, V. (1994). *Making sense of secondary science: Research into children's ideas.* London, England: Routledge.

[3] Geelan, D. R. (1997). Epistemological anarchy and the many forms of constructivism. *Science & Education, 6,* 15–28.

[4] Tobin, K. (1993). Preface: Constructivism: A paradigm for the practice of science education. In K. Tobin (Ed.), *The practice of constructivism in science education* (pp. ix–xvi). Hillsdale, NJ: Lawrence Erlbaum Associates.

[5] Ashton, P. (1984). Teacher efficacy: A motivational paradigm for effective teacher education. *Journal of Teacher Education, 35*(5), 28–32.

[6] Ashton, P. (1984). Teacher efficacy: A motivational paradigm for effective teacher education. *Journal of Teacher Education, 35*(5), 29.

[7] Manktelow, J., & Carlson, A. (2015). *Questioning techniques: Video transcript.* Retrieved from https://www.mindtools.com/pages/article/newTMC_88.htm

[8] Exploratorium Institute for Inquiry. (2006). *Assessing for learning: Workshops designed to introduce teachers to formative assessment* (Workshops I–IV). San Francisco, CA. Retrieved from www.exploratorium.edu/ifi/workshops/assessing/

[9] Berkeley University of California Center for Teaching and Learning. (2015). *Student engagement: Asking and answering questions.* Retrieved from http://teaching.berkeley.edu/asking-and-answering-questions

[10] Gallas, K. (1995). *Talking their way into science: Hearing children's questions and theories, responding with curricula.* New York, NY: Teachers College Press.

[11] National Science Teachers Association. (2014). *Common elementary student science misconceptions.* Retrieved from http://www.nsta.org/elementaryschool/connections/201209AppropriateTopics-ElementaryStudentScienceMisconceptions.pdf

STEP THREE

Create a Learning Atmosphere

I hear, and I forget, I see, and I remember, I do, and I understand.

Chinese Proverb

An optimal classroom setting for success in teaching and learning science creates and embraces an atmosphere that is:

- positive;
- cheerful;
- optimistic;
- constructive;
- practical;
- investigative;
- analytical;
- inspiring;
- engaging;
- safe.

As stated above, the Chinese proverb best sums up the principles of inquiry-based learning. "Inquiry implies involvement that leads to understanding. Furthermore, involvement in learning implies possessing skills and attitudes that permit you to seek resolutions to questions and issues while you construct new knowledge."[1]

Scientists generally follow the same path as they study things and try to figure out patterns or rules to explain how something works. Using inquiry to solve a problem, they ask questions, investigate through observations and experimentation, collect and organize data, and then solve problems based on their prior knowledge and the evidence they have gathered. Bass et al.[2] agree, "...if teachers view science as inquiry and children as constructive learners, they will want to teach science in ways that engage students in the active construction of ideas and explanations and enhance their abilities to inquire." Therefore, teachers should provide a learning atmosphere where students have ample opportunities to engage in the process of learning and, at the same time, mirror the behavior of scientists.

DEFINING EXPECTATIONS

What is inquiry-based learning? How do you incorporate it into your classroom curriculum? Into your classroom management plan? To answer these questions, I suggest you take a look at Step Five, which explains it in detail. For now, keep in mind the following:

- Create a conducive and engaging environment for learning, one in which students feel comfortable and self-confident.
- Make students aware of your expectations.
- Be cognizant of students' ability to meet your expectations.
- Set the classroom rules from the onset, the first day of class.
- Expect students to work toward their potential and to always "do their best."
- Let them express their ideas and opinions as they learn to work with others.

While teaching a thematic unit on birds for a third grade class, Greenspan[3] noted that her students:

> …took pride in sharing what they knew, conveying their enthusiasm. Entering into discussion with preconceived ideas and various experiences, the children quickly altered their constructs and created new ones based on the opportunity to engage, inquire, and communicate with each other. Soon, the students were in control of their own learning and looked to me as the guide rather than the sage in their quest for new knowledge.

A DISCIPLINED APPROACH

One way to create a positive learning atmosphere involves developing a good, workable classroom management plan. Many approaches to discipline exist, but I prefer a form of Assertive Discipline,[4] which sets expectations and limitations and allows students to develop the rules and plan of action with the teacher. Briefly, this is a structured plan, but democratic in nature, which enhances the environment as a cooperative learning experience in which students are engaged throughout the learning process and are aware of exactly what the teacher expects of them. Conversely, the teacher knows what to expect of her students. Kaufenberg[5] agrees that assertive teachers are confident and quick in all types of situations that require behavior management. She further claims that in this environment, there are few rules, but they are stated clearly and firmly. Positive reinforcement is given to those who follow the rules, while there are consequences for those who do not abide by the rules.

As an example, on the first day of school, the students and I brainstorm about four to five easy-to-follow classroom rules and the consequences if the rules are not obeyed. Depending on the grade level, one student copies the rules onto a poster board, which you display in the classroom at all times throughout the school year. Students are given three chances to redirect their behavior, and if they do not comply they have to confront the first consequence. We then agree on three to four consequences, which have been discussed, outlined, and posted, along with the rules of the classroom. In my classroom, I keep a pad of paper close by so I can keep an ongoing log, recording both positive and negative behaviors of students. I refer to it as needed.

Of course, it is important for teachers to consistently apply consequences based on negative behavior, but it's equally important to regularly reward good behavior. Incentives such as stickers, smiley faces, or letters to parents, or simply smiles, pats on the back, or "high fives," encourage good behavior. Likewise, applying your previously outlined consequences to the behavior that does not follow the rules is a disincentive. Your goal is to provide an efficient and effective place for learning:

> More than being a director, assertive teachers build positive, trusting relationships with their students and teach appropriate classroom behavior (via direct instruction ... describing, modeling, practicing, reviewing, encouraging, and rewarding) to those who don't show it at present. They are demanding, yet warm in interaction; supportive of the youngsters; and respectful in tone and mannerisms when addressing misbehavior. Assertive teachers listen carefully to what their students have to say, speak politely to them, and treat everyone fairly (not necessarily equally).[6]

CLASSROOM CONFIGURATION

The layout of the classroom is another key factor for creating a productive and upbeat learning atmosphere that also enhances cooperative learning (discussed further in Step Seven). Tables and/or desks should be arranged in a group setting with five students at each table. If this is untenable, because of the number of students or furniture availability issues, then students should be able to conduct their investigations by simply moving their desks into this formation during science learning times. The teacher's desk should be strategically located, enabling teachers to observe students working individually, in small group settings, or as a whole group; however, it shouldn't be the focal point within the classroom. If possible, you should have a table or counter for manipulatives that might be needed for particular lessons, plus you might want water readily available. Regardless of grade level, students should be aware they are responsible for cleanup and storage of the science tools after conducting their experiments. Place bulletin board displays of students' work, posters, pictures, classroom rules, and other visual products throughout the classroom.

SAFETY IN YOUR CLASSROOM

Creating an effective science learning atmosphere also requires obeying certain safety procedures. It goes without saying that you should demonstrate and model safe behavior and discuss safety procedures and regulations with students prior to learning. Additionally, you should have access to a telephone within your classroom for emergencies.[7] The National Science Teachers Association lists many rules that apply to the upper grades. However, the following would apply to elementary students. They should:

- Wear gloves when needed;
- Use goggles, safety glasses, and possible aprons when using substances that could be harmful;
- Always experiment under adult supervision;
- Dress appropriately so that your clothes do not interfere with your investigation;
- Listen to teachers' directions.[8]

Of course, there are many other things to consider, but for purposes of this guidebook, think about the overall impression of your classroom. To anyone entering your classroom, it should suggest a warm, secure, safe, trusting place of learning. It's a place where teacher and students respect one another and conduct themselves in an organized, engaging, and constructive learning environment.

KEY POINTS

- Implement inquiry-based learning, where students are given opportunities to become a community of learners engaged toward a common goal.
- Develop a structured classroom management plan in which students know the rules and are expected to follow them, and you are aware of their ability to adhere to them.
- Create a classroom layout that encourages hands-on learning.
- Follow important safety guidelines.

NOTES

[1] Exline, J. (2004). *Concept to classroom: Workshop: Inquiry-based learning* (p. 1). Retrieved from http://www.thirteen.org/edonline/concept2class/inquiry/index.html
[2] Bass, J. E., Contant, T. L., & Carin, A. A. (2009). *Methods for teaching science as inquiry* (p. 3). Boston, MA: Pearson Education, Inc.
[3] Greenspan, Y. F. (1999). Scientific inquiry: A journey for a teacher and students. In T. L. Kielborn & P. J. Gilmer (Eds.), *Meaningful science: Teachers doing inquiry + teaching science* (p. 91). Tallahassee, FL: SERVE.
[4] Canter, L., & Canter, M., (2001). *Assertive discipline: Positive behavior management for today's classroom* (3rd ed.). Los Angeles, CA: Canter & Associates.
[5] Kaufenberg, J. (2013). *Assertive discipline: A systematic approach.* Retrieved from http://assertivedisciplineclassroommanagement.pbworks.com/w/page/54424891/Canter%27s%20 Assertive%20Discipline%20Model

[6] Canter, L., & Canter, M. (2014). *Assertive discipline* (p. 1). Retrieved from http://www.behavioradvisor.com/AssertiveDiscipline.html

[7] Center for Educator Development in Fine Arts. (2015). *Safety in the classroom.* Retrieved from http://www.cedfa.org/teach-fine-arts/instruction/safety-in-the-classroom/

[8] National Science Teachers Association. (2015). *Safety in the science classroom.* Retrieved from http://www.nsta.org/docs/SafetyInTheScienceClassroom.pdf

STEP FOUR

Integrate the Curriculum

Teachers inspire students to dream, and give them the tools and knowledge to make those dreams come true.[1]

The acronym STEM refers to the academic disciplines of *science, technology, engineering,* and *mathematics*, and defined as:

> STEM education is an interdisciplinary approach to learning where rigorous academic concepts are coupled with real world lessons as students apply science, technology, engineering, and mathematics in contexts that make connections between school, community, work, and the global enterprise enabling the development of STEM literacy and with it the ability to compete in the new economy.[2]

The objective of grouping these disciplines is to encourage teachers to emphasize these fields and promote formal and informal lessons that elicit problem-solving and advance student potential. According to the National Science Board, "The Nation needs 'STEM innovators' – those individuals who have developed the expertise to become leading STEM professionals and perhaps the creators of significant breakthroughs or advances in scientific and technological understanding."[3]

WHY INTEGRATE THE DISCIPLINES?

Specifically, in this step, we discuss how to integrate science with other curricula, such as language arts, mathematics, social studies, art, and engineering. (The issue of integrating technology is addressed in depth in Step Eight.)

Although it may seem that integrating the disciplines is a complicated undertaking, in reality it saves teachers' planning time, strengthens and combines content, reinforces skills in other subjects, and develops a connection between several curricula areas. Integrating subject areas also makes science more real, which we hope gives students the skills and knowhow to solve life's problems.

INTEGRATING LANGUAGE ARTS

"Literacy skills are critical to building knowledge in science." So says the Next Generation Standards in 2013.[4] Embedded in the Common Core Standards (CSS), the essential skills of reading and writing in English Language Arts (ELA) are currently moving toward integrating with the Next Generation Science Standards (NGSS). This connects the content of both, especially for science students, and aids in understanding the nature of science and gathering evidence, making and assessing solutions, and synthesizing complex concepts.

In language arts, the goal is to develop the full range of students' literacy skills, including speaking, listening, reading, and writing. By integrating these skills into the science learning process, students gain a better understanding of the subject matter. For example, reading stories from children's storybooks or creating science Word Walls to enhance vocabulary sparks interest and motivates students to want to learn more.

Student journaling is another way to improve literacy skills and only takes five minutes a day or so. Generally, students can write in a small notebook or on single sheets of paper that are given to the teacher and assessed either daily, biweekly, or monthly. Journaling may be ongoing throughout the school year or simply written/drawn as a day-to-day entry. Regardless, this time is set aside to reflect on previous science experiences or to write what was learned that day in science. Sometimes, the teacher can provide a question or statement that the student has to answer or write about in a certain amount of time. At other times, students simply write what they are thinking about in science, reflecting on their ideas without time constraints. Some teacher-created questions could include:

- How are push and pull different?
- Describe the water cycle.
- Describe how the earth revolves around the sun.
- Draw the solar system.
- Why do we have seasons on Earth?
- Write about the three kinds of rocks.
- Why is recycling important?
- Write about the patterns you see in stars.
- Write about the food chain.
- How are living and non-living animals different? Similar?
- How are mass and weight different? Similar?

Similarly, teachers could provide writing prompts that allow students to focus on both their language arts and science skills. The following websites suggest writing prompts appropriate for science learning:

- http://www.creative-writing-ideas-and-activities.com/science-writing-prompts.html
- http://www.myteacherpages.com/webpages/jgriffin/files/Science%20Journal%20Topics.pdf

Science notebooks are simply a compilation of students' journal entries designed to inform the teacher of the student's understanding of a scientific concept(s). For all grade levels, science notebook entries can be written in either prose or drawn in pictures or both. As stated above, you can use a science notebook for journaling or, more informally, individual sheets of paper can be completed and compiled. If you use a science journal for grades kindergarten, first, and second, it's best to use large drawing paper you've stapled together; at these young ages, children's hands are still too small to handle the perforated spiral black/white notebooks.

Science notebooks can be as creative as you like, and could include 3-dimensional drawings, glued objects, reports, research, foldables, note taking, and charts/graphs/diagrams. Students may wish to address their feelings about certain science misconceptions, their interpretations of evidence, and/or personal reflections about a specific science topic.

Overall, notebooks are an excellent strategy for students to communicate their science knowledge. They may be used before, during or after an investigation; in other words, notebooks are an effective format for teachers to learn what individual students know and need to know.

Incorporating graphic organizers is another excellent approach that integrates language arts' skills and further creates interest in science. For more than thirty years, Project CRISS (Creating Independence through Student-owned Strategies) has been assisting students in reading. Designed as an educational initiative, which embeds the Common Core Standards and the Next Generation Standards, CRISS helps students of all abilities learn content across the curriculum and throughout the grade levels.[5] By incorporating some of Project CRISS' instructional practices and practical tools in science, we see students' reading skills improved and reinforced, as science content becomes more meaningful.

The following are just a few examples of CRISS strategies:[6]

Figure 2. Spider map. Write the scientific concept in the center of the circle (the body of the spider), generate appropriate questions on the topic, and record students' responses on the lines (spider legs). Discuss and review

21

Observations	Inferences

Figure 3. T-chart or two column chart. Students organize ideas by listing their thoughts. It can also be adapted to a Three-Column or Four-Column Chart

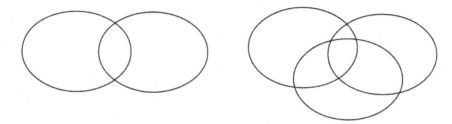

Figure 4. Venn diagrams. Compare and contrast two or three views of a science concept, such as what attracts magnets and what repels magnets. Write students' responses in each circle. In the middle circle, write what those views have in common. Complete same for the three-circled diagram

What I Know	What I Want to Know	What I Learned

Figure 5. K-W-L chart. Students respond to the first two columns prior to teaching the concept and record their responses. The third column is completed after students learn the concept

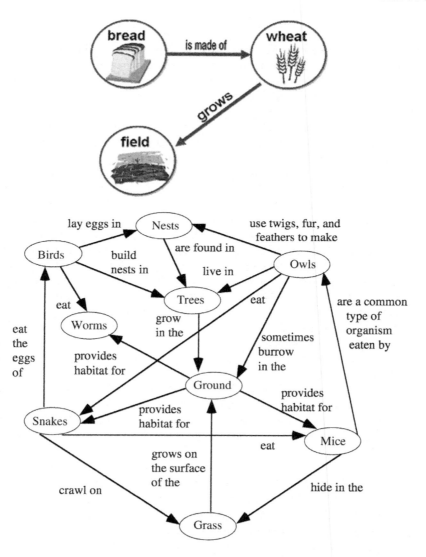

Figure 6. Concept mapping for primary and intermediate grades.[7]
Concept Mapping is a visual representation consisting of concepts and
a labeled line with a phrase that describes the relationship between a pair
of concepts that connect that line, using a verb to do the connection. Together,
the two concepts and labeled line that connects them represent a unit
of knowledge, a proposition, or linking phrase[8]

INTEGRATING MATHEMATICS

"Science is a quantitative discipline, so it is important for educators to ensure that students' science learning coheres well with their learning in mathematics."[9] Therefore, it is equally important to integrate mathematics into your science curriculum. The National Mathematics Content Standards include such skills as numbers and operations, algebra, geometry, measurement, data analysis, and probability.[10] Science and mathematics complement each other because the character of both disciplines conveys a world of patterns that repeat in a predictable fashion and are arranged because they follow a certain rule or rules.

Here's an example: In a simple classroom investigation, such as inferring and observing the properties of three kinds of white powder, students measure a certain amount of each powder with a certain measurable amount of liquid (water or iodide, commonly known as iodine).They mix them together and determine the name of the powder. Once they record results in a chart/graph, they analyze their findings, linking both mathematics and science to reinforce learning (see Lesson Plan, *Mystery Powder*). We ask ourselves, then, how can mathematics not be included in the progression of conducting an experiment? How can the skills of measuring, numbers and operations, and data analysis not be emphasized? How can one observe patterns in mathematics and not in science and vice versa?

"For purposes of general scientific literacy, it is important for students (1) to understand in what sense mathematics is the study of patterns and relationships, (2) to become familiar with some of those patterns and relationships, and (3) to learn to use them in daily life."[11]

Indeed, patterns are everywhere around us. Mathematical and scientific patterns are even highlighted and addressed in the Benchmarks for Science Literacy by the American Association for the Advancement of Science (AAAS) in 1993[12] and listed as one of the seven crosscutting concepts in the Next Generation Science Standards in April, 2013.[13]

By using mathematical manipulatives and searching for patterns in the process of solving a problem, students gain a better understanding of scientific concepts and at the same time, sharpen their mathematical skills. Gilmer[14] remarks that as a biochemist researching the topic of cell-cell interactions and a system, she found that: "…for the entire time I was looking for patterns in nature, seeing one part, and then as I learned more, seeing a bigger part of the pattern, all the while undergoing paradigm shifts in my thinking and understanding."

We want our students to model scientists, who learn to solve problems based on how and what they observe in their world, by testing evidence, noting patterns, constructing explanations, and drawing conclusions from what they perceive. "Children are cognizant of patterns in their environment. They observe them in the designs of their clothes, in daily routines and simple chores, and even in the natural phenomena of nature, such as veins on leaves, color of animals and bodies of insects."[15]

A teacher should provide ample activities for students to infer, predict, and observe patterns. This could involve:

- viewing an ecosystem;
- examining cells in a microscope;
- taking photos on a nature walk;
- drawing veins of a leaf;
- studying the parts of a flower;
- observing camouflage patterns of animals;
- watching the feeding habits or listening to the language sounds of primates or other animals.

These activities give students opportunities to visualize, view, and identify patterns or sequential designs within nature, which, in the long term, helps them organize their world[16] and facilitates learning.

INTEGRATING SOCIAL STUDIES

Social studies is the study of cultural, economic, political, and environmental issues. How natural to integrate it with science and help students make connections to their everyday lives! By joining these two disciplines, students gain a better understanding of who they are in the world where they live. As a teacher, the curriculum invites you to plan lessons or units of study that integrate these subjects. For instance, if the curriculum revolves around animals, you could provide world maps that show where the animals live and what kind of habitat they require, including the impact of flora and fauna on their ability to survive (see Appendix IV). Students could study the history of an area and learn about the people who lived there in the past and identify those living there now. In the upper grades, students could explore world population and their food supplies, identifying locations of pertinent countries on a world map.

If you're fortunate to live near a national, state, or county park, students could study the surrounding terrain of the habitats. For example, they could learn how the land affects them in their community by exploring the weather patterns, rainfall, and global warming effects on a particular area. They could also study famous scientists from around the world and learn how their contribution to science influenced their communities and the world. The possibilities are limitless. Just think of patterns that affect the earth's surface, such as, erosion and weathering, earthquakes, tsunamis, hurricanes, and tornadoes. Students could create timelines, concept mapping, and dioramas or posters to enhance their appreciation and understanding of how geographical and historical phenomena are linked to scientific concepts.

INTEGRATING ART

In a world of art that incorporates science, patterns also exist. We see patterns in moving molecules, in cell formation, and in architectural designs. Students should

25

integrate art and science into their daily activities by sketching, drawing, or painting what they have learned in science. In addition, they could also read and study planets, and then draw their shapes and sizes while noting the pattern in the planets' orbit. They could create three-dimensional accounts of a science concept, draw a cartoon of an animal's habitat, or they could work together in collaborative groups to produce science announcements, advertisements, posters, and experience charts.

Crafting is another form of linking art and science. Students could make Paper Mache or clay planets and paint them, for example, or they could create water cycle bracelets with various colors of small beads: yellow for solar energy, clear for evaporation, green for transpiration, white for condensation, and blue for precipitation (see Lesson Plan, Learning about the Water Cycle). These are just two ideas through which teachers can integrate science and art.

INTEGRATING ENGINEERING

Let's not forget to include lessons in engineering skills, where students have the opportunity to design, build, and test simple bridges, machines, and other structures that use everyday materials, such as discarded toilet paper rolls, toothpicks, tongue depressors, Popsicle sticks, and straws.

Through critical thinking, students learn to identify and solve simple engineering designs as shown in Figure 7 below. "Students begin a design challenge; the early design fails, creating a need for scientific knowledge; the knowledge is acquired

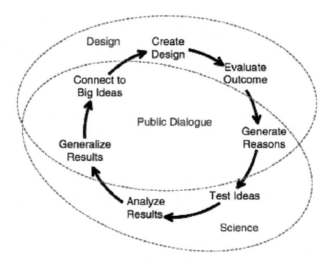

Figure 7. Engineering design. First, students create a design, evaluate its outcome, generate reasons for its validity, test their ideas, analyze and generalize their results, and connect their design to other big ideas[17]

through experimentation and reading; and the design task is resumed, with new scientific knowledge in hand."[18] As students work together to plan and create their engineering models (see Lesson Plans, *Engineering Design*) you will soon observe them talking the language of science and sharing ideas on how to construct a feasible representation of a structure they may see in their environment.

As you can see, we have barely scratched the surface of the vast possibilities for integrating various subject areas into your classroom science teaching.

KEY POINTS

- Ask yourself how you can help your students derive a better understanding of the dynamic nature of science?
- Recognize that integrating language arts, mathematics, social studies, art, and engineering design is an effective way to enhance your everyday science teaching.
- Realize that even if your lessons configure only one or two other subject areas into your science classroom, you are enhancing your students' learning.

NOTES

[1] Weisskirch, R. (2011, October 17). *Sharing teaching resources and making SRA stronger* (p. 8). Retrieved from http://www.s-r-a.org/search/node/Teachers%20inspire%20students

[2] Tsupros, N. (2009). *Southwest Pennsylvania STEM network long range plan (2009–2018): Plan summary* (p. 3). Retrieved from http://business-leadershipcoaching.com/wp-content/uploads/2013/08/SWP-STEM-STRATEGY-Final-Report-Summary-July-2009.pdf

[3] The National Science Board. (2010, May 5). *Preparing the next generation of STEM educators: Identifying and developing our nation's human capital* (p. 1). Retrieved from http://www.nsf.gov/nsb/publications/2010/nsb1033_exec_summary.pdf

[4] Next Generation Science Standards. (2013, May). *Appendix M: Connections to the common core state standards for literacy in science and technical subjects* (p. 1). Retrieved from http://ngss.nsta.org/documents/AppendixM-

[5] Project CRISS. (2014). Retrieved from http://www.projectcriss.com/

[6] Santa, C. M., Havens, L. T., & Valdes, B. J. (2004). *Creating independence through student-owned strategies* (3rd ed.). Dubuque, IA: Kendall/Hunt Publishing Company.

[7] Images for Concept Mapping. (2015). Retrieved from https://www.google.com/search?q=concept+mapping&biw=1280&bih=595&tbm=isch&tbo=u&source=univ&sa=X&ved=0CF0QsARqFQoTCImxwvmeicgCFQarHgod_LMH1w&dpr=1.25

[8] Greenspan, Y. F. (2011, Fall). *Concept mapping* [PowerPoint slides]. Retrieved from Miami Dade College lecture.

[9] Next Generation Science Standards. (2013, May). *Appendix L: Connections to the common core state standards for mathematics* (p. 1). Retrieved from http://www.nextgenscience.org/sites/ngss/files/Appendix-L_CCSS%20Math%20Connections%2006_03_13.pdf

[10] The National Council for Accreditation of Teacher Education (NCATE) and National Council of Teachers of Mathematics (NCTM) Program Standards. (2003). *Program standards for initial preparation of mathematics teachers: Standards for secondary mathematics teachers*. Retrieved from http://www.nctm.org/uploadedFiles/Standards_and_Positions/CAEP_Standards/NCTMSECONStandards.pdf

[11] Benchmarks On-Line (2015). *The nature of mathematics: Patterns and relationships* (p. 1). Retrieved from http://www.project2061.org/publications/bsl/online/index.php?chapter=2

[12] American Association for the Advancement of Science (AAAS). (1993). *Benchmarks for science literacy*. New York, NY: Oxford University Press, Inc.

[13] Next Generation Science Standards. (2013, April). *Appendix G: Crosscutting concepts*. Retrieved from www.nextgenscience.org/sites/ngss/files/Appendix%20G%20-%20Crosscutting%20Concepts%20 FINAL%20edited%204.10.13.pdf

[14] Gilmer, P. J. (1999). *Looking at science as a pattern: Learning from differing perspectives* (p. 5). Presented at the annual meeting, National Association for Research in Science Teaching, Boston, MA.

[15] Greenspan, Y. F. (1999). *A community of learners: Linking scientific patterns of life* (p. 3). Presented at the annual meeting, National Association for Research in Science Teaching, Boston, MA.

[16] Greenspan, Y. F. (1999). *A community of learners: Linking scientific patterns of life* (p. 3). Presented at the annual meeting, National Association for Research in Science Teaching, Boston, MA.

[17] Schunn, C. D. (2009, Fall). How kids learn engineering: The cognitive science perspective. *The Bridge, 39*(3), 35. Retrieved from https://www.nae.edu/Publications/Bridge/16145/16214.aspx

[18] Schunn, C. D. (2009, Fall). How kids learn engineering: The cognitive science perspective. *The Bridge, 39*(3), 34. Retrieved from https://www.nae.edu/Publications/Bridge/16145/16214.aspx

STEP FIVE

Engage the Learner

More and more jobs demand advanced skills, requiring that people be able to learn, reason, think creatively, make decisions, and solve problems. An understanding of science and the processes of science contributes in an essential way to these skills.[1]

Research indicates that engaging students in the learning process increases their focus and attention and helps motive them to apply higher level critical thinking skills.[2] Engaging and challenging your students is an important and difficult task. However, delivering lessons that are well-planned, inspiring, and full of surprises is a path to creating students eager to learn. After all, our ultimate goal is to motivate students to become active learners.

According to the previously mentioned Constructivist Theory of Learning, students generate knowledge through an interaction with their experiences. In other words, students construct their own knowledge; it is an active process of generating meaning for the science concept.[3] The key term is *active learning*, whereby the student is an active participant and connected to what is being taught.

GRAB THEIR ATTENTION

How do we reach the goal of active learning? From the beginning of the lesson, teachers should create an atmosphere of energy, passion, and enthusiasm for the concept. In this atmosphere, the teacher's role is no longer limited to dispensing "truth" and knowledge but rather transforms into one that helps and guides the learner in the conceptual organization of certain areas of experience.[4] Teachers should grab the attention of all their students, thereby supporting them in the learning process.

We can accomplish this simply by including activities that encourage students to respond to your open-ended, critical thinking questions or have them elicit their own questions about the concept. Incorporate prompts or tools that focus on the concept and simultaneously promote active learning. Get everyone involved. Allow students to explore and discover together; give them opportunities to share their ideas and opinions with each other and with you.

In my article describing the way students can learn about migrating birds, I said:

> By incorporating hands-on, minds-on activities, I augmented basic skills and integrated science process skills/practices. Basic skills – like observing, communicating, classifying, measuring, inferring, and predicting – led students to exhibit curiosity, questioning, and interpretations of the world around them[5] (see Step Seven).

INQUIRY-BASED LEARNING

There are several methods that promote students to become active learners, to investigate and discover as they proceed to learn. For the purposes of this guidebook, inquiry-based instruction appears to be the most effective and valuable method to promote independent learning, defined as: a learner who can research and create questions about a scientific concept and expand upon it based on gathered evidence. Bond states, "Inquiry learning is an approach that provides learners opportunities to actively develop skills that enable them to locate, gather, analyze, critique and apply information in a wide range of contexts, as they develop understanding."[6] He further states that when implementing inquiry effectively, the following conditions are usually met or there is evidence of progress:

- students are actively supported and scaffolded by teachers in the acquisition of relevant skills,
- students are engaged in learning,
- students deepen or gain understanding of core concepts relevant to the context,
- students work collaboratively in small groups,
- students use and apply the information then share their solutions, decisions, thinking and outcomes in a celebration of understanding. They are not involved in a process of shifting and sharing information,
- students will access a range of information sources, students predicate their work on prior knowledge, [and]
- students will be actively engaged in asking and following up on questions as a central skill.[7]

BECOMING EMPOWERED

As a result of implementing an inquiry-based learning environment, students become empowered and are allowed to be in charge, so to speak, of their own learning. Scaffolding is a term that employs a variety of instructional strategies that move students toward stronger understanding, greater independence, and also allows them to acquire more skills and reach higher levels of comprehension.[8] Eventually, the teacher gradually shifts more responsibility of the learning process to the student. Such an environment generates positive achievement and success. Consequently, the classroom becomes student-oriented rather than teacher-oriented, which in turn promotes a sense of student ownership. In this atmosphere, both teachers and students are aware of the expectations. As Erwin explains, belonging, power, freedom, and fun provide an all encompassing learning environment with the goal of exacting a quality classroom environment. He further states: "Unless the students understand specifically what is expected of them and how the expectations benefit them, there is little chance they will be motivated to meet those expectations."[9]

THREE APPROACHES OF INQUIRY-BASED LEARNING

Inquiry-based learning is accomplished through three different approaches. The teacher must decide which approach would be most advantageous given students' abilities, preconceived notions, and/or experiences with the science concept. Each approach is based on the degree of students' involvement in the process of inquiry, the degree or amount of time the teacher intervenes in instructing the students, the students' scientific background with the inquiry subject, and relevant working methods.[10]

First, structured inquiry is essentially directed by the teacher, and may be the scientific method or other similar processes. The teacher determines:

- the exact directions given to the students;
- the precise issues to be research and solved.

In addition:

- the teacher closely supervises the learning process; and
- students must explain and justify their explanation based on the evidence they have collected.[11]

In using inquiry-based learning, "The teacher provides students with a hands-on problem to investigate, as well as the procedures, and materials, but does not inform them of expected outcomes. Students are to discover relationships between variables or otherwise generalize from data collected."[12]

With the guided inquiry process, the student also becomes slightly more independent. Students design their procedure to test their question and their explanations. In this process:

- teachers provide the problem for investigation;
- teachers provide the necessary materials;
- students are expected to devise their own procedure to solve the problem.[13]

Colburn suggests, "The teacher provides only the materials and problem to investigate. Students devise their own procedure to solve the problem."[14]

Finally, in open-inquiry, there is no prescribed target, and instead:

- students formulate and create their own problem to investigate and solve;
- students design their question;
- students carry out the investigation;

- students communicate their results;
- students work collaboratively to discover results; and
- teachers guide them toward the learning goal without making it obvious or explicit.[15]

Open inquiry learning best mirrors what scientists do day to day, in that learners use heightened cognitive skills and increased scientific reasoning.

THE 5-E INSTRUCTIONAL MODEL

Although there are other models for inquiry-based learning, I believe the 5-E Instructional Model (5Es), in which students have opportunities to build new ideas on top of their old ones, best connects the learner to the science concept and helps the process of conceptual change. As a result, students develop an understanding of the nature of science and learn to develop practical and teamwork skills.[16]

The 5Es each represent a phase of learning. They are:

- Engage – the teacher accesses the students' prior knowledge and engages them in the learning with an exciting introduction of the concept.
- Explore – the students are given opportunities to explore in an activity.
- Explain – the students explain what they have learned about the concept.
- Elaborate – the students' understanding of the concept is challenged and further expanded from their new experiences.
- Evaluate – the students assess their understanding of the concept.[17,18]

As we plan our science lessons, we should take into account that the 5Es don't necessarily need to be taught in sequential order and, at times, each phase overlaps with another.

EXAMPLES USING THE 5-E INSTRUCTIONAL MODEL

The nature of matter is a concept that is covered in both primary and intermediate grades, as well as secondary grades. Learning about the three states of matter (liquids, solids, gases) evolves from a simple one taught in kindergarten to a more multifaceted one presented in fifth grade to a more sophisticated topic in secondary grades. Using inquiry learning, begin the engagement phase by generating questions that ask students what they know and what they want to know. Try to eliminate students' misconceptions or misunderstandings about the concept.

Next, in the exploration stage, give your students opportunities to explore the properties of liquids, solids, and gases by observing different liquids or smelling vinegar or touching different solids, such as cotton or blocks of wood. Have students monitor how liquids can change from one state to another, such as ice to water and vice versa. For the final phases of explanation, elaboration, and evaluation, let students explain what they have investigated, justifying their results, and communicating and sharing it with each other. For the young student, this can be accomplished with drawings, singing songs, or creating booklets. Older students can create skits, design their own investigation, or write a story.

As another example, we can use the 5-E Instructional Model to teach electricity. During the engagement phase, introduce the topic either in a whole or small group discussion, and ask critical thinking questions that encourage all students to express what they know about the concept. For example, you could ask: What is electricity? How does it occur? Why do we need electricity? Employ open-ended questioning techniques, ones that begin with How or Why, which force critical thinking.

Next, in the exploration phase, you could have students use a simple piece of foil-wrapped masking tape about twelve inches long and one inch wide, along with a miniature light bulb and D battery, to discover through trial and error how to light the bulb. Students also could design electrical circuit boards on cardboard sheets with everyday wires and batteries.

Finally, in the explanation, elaboration, and evaluation phases, the students could create a group project on electricity to share with other classmates.

Keep in mind that most lesson plans for any given grade level can be adapted to the age group of students in your classroom and adjusted to meet the standards and requirements of the curriculum. However, the basic lesson plan framework remains the same.

TEACH *ALL* LEARNERS

In addition, teachers should be aware of the many different kinds of learners. It's the implicit task of all teachers to direct instruction to *all* learners. You can accomplish this by appealing to many different learning styles during a lesson. For example, teachers can implement differentiated instruction strategies, such as tailoring and accessing science content based on what students need to learn. This gives them opportunities to master content through engaging activities, and allows them to apply and extend what has been learned in final projects. In this way, students, whether individually or in small groups, receive the best learning experience possible.[19] For example, since some students are auditory learners, teachers can provide tools such as videos or CDs that encourage these students to learn by listening. Others are visual learners, so teachers can consider using a variety of visuals, such as posters, drawings, charts, graphs, computer-generated presentations, real-life pictures or photographs. Finally, we need to think about students who learn only through tactile strategies, and provide hands-on manipulatives to use to experiment, model, and discover.

It's possible to include strategies for all three learning styles in every lesson, thus, simultaneously motivating audio, visual, and tactile learners and encouraging their natural curiosity. As a result, students become independent, confident learners willing to take responsibility for their own learning.

SUMMING UP

As a lesson evolves from the beginning to the end, the teacher should strive to create an atmosphere that demonstrates a love of learning, taking into consideration what students already know and guiding them in the direction of their interests. Incorporating inquiry learning encourages students to solve problems together, collect evidence, and communicate results. Jeanpierre[20] states, "Inquiry is at the heart of scientific thinking." Teachers facilitating inquiry in their classrooms that sparks students' curiosity are central in helping those students develop "scientific habits of mind." The ultimate goal is "more than simply helping students to understand scientific principles and theories, science teachers empower students to think and to solve problems that will emerge in the future... Passionate science teachers create classrooms of discovery that model excitement for their field and learning."[21]

KEY POINTS

- To achieve active learning, it's necessary for teachers to focus on ways to engage their students.
- Inquiry-based learning is a pathway to engaging students in active learning.
- The 5-E Instructional Model is one of the best ways to facilitate inquiry-based learning; the 5Es are engage, explore, explain, elaborate, and evaluate.
- An inquiry-based learning model helps teachers engage all their students regardless of learning style.

NOTES

[1] National Committee on Science Education Standards and National Research Council. (1996). *National science education standards* (p. 1). Retrieved from http://www.nap.edu/openbook.php?record_id=4962&page=1

[2] University of Washington: Center for Teaching and Learning. (2015). *Engaging students in learning.* Retrieved from http://www.washington.edu/teaching/teaching-resources/engaging-students-in-learning/

[3] Guba, E. G., & Lincoln, Y. S. (1989). *Fourth generation evaluation.* Newbury Park, CA: Sage Publications.

[4] von Glaserfeld, E. (1988). *Environment and communication.* Paper presented at Sixth International Congress on Mathematics Education, Budapest, Hungary.

[5] Greenspan, Y. F. (1999). *Meaningful science: Teachers doing inquiry + teaching science* (p. 90). Tallahassee, FL: SERVE.

[6] Bond, T. (2011, June). *Inquiry learning* (p. 1). Retrieved from http://ictnz.com/Inquiry%20Learning/inquirydefinition.htm

[7] Bond, T. (2011, June). *Inquiry learning* (p. 1). Retrieved from http://ictnz.com/Inquiry%20Learning/inquirydefinition.htm

[8] Glossary of Education Reform. (2015, April 6). *Scaffolding.* Retrieved from http://edglossary.org/scaffolding/

[9] Erwin, J. C. (2004). *The classroom of choice: Giving students what they need and getting what you want* (Chapter 4, p. 1). Alexandria, VA: Association for Supervision and Curriculum Developed. Retrieved from http://www.ascd.org/publications/books/104020/chapters/Power-in-the-Classroom@-Creating-the-Environment.aspx

[10] Sadeh, I., & Zion, M. (2009, December). The development of dynamic inquiry performances within an open inquiry setting: A comparison to guided inquiry setting. *Journal of Research in Science Teaching, 46*, 1137–1160.

[11] Beacon Learning Center. (1997). *Just science now.* Retrieved from http://www.justsciencenow.com/about.htm

[12] Colburn, A. (2000, March). *An inquiry primer* (p. 1). Retrieved from www.ubclts.com/docs/Inquiry_Primer.pdf

[13] Beacon Learning Center. (1997). *Just science now.* Retrieved from http://www.justsciencenow.com/

[14] Colburn, A. (2000, March). *An inquiry primer* (p. 1). Retrieved from www.ubclts.com/docs/Inquiry_Primer.pdf

[15] Beacon Learning Center. (1997). Retrieved from http://www.justsciencenow.com/

[16] BSCS 5E Instructional Model. (2012). Retrieved from http://www.bscs.org/bscs-5e-instructional-model

[17] BSCS 5E Instructional Model. (2012). Retrieved from http://www.bscs.org/bscs-5e-instructional-model

[18] Enhancing Education. (2002). *The 5e's.* Retrieved http://enhancinged.wgbh.org/research/eeeee.html

[19] Tomlinson, C. A. (2000, August). Differentiation of instruction in the elementary grades. *ERIC Digest.* Champaign, IL: ERIC Clearinghouse on Elementary and Early Childhood Education. Retrieved from http://www.readingrockets.org/article/what-differentiated-instruction

[20] Jeanpierrre, B. (2014, January). Inquiry in the urban science classroom: Connecting curiosity and creativity. *NSTA Reports, 25*(5), 3.

[21] Duncan, A. (2011). Educated the opinions: Science education and knowledge economy. *NSTA Reports, 22*(9), 3.

STEP SIX

Assemble Your Materials

The scientist is not a person who gives the right answers, he's one who asks the right questions.

Claude Lévi-Strauss

One of the most difficult crossroads in teaching a worthy science curriculum relates to the materials you use, the tools that students use to explore and discover. On the one hand, gathering the necessary materials to help you implement an inquiry-based learning program can be frustrating, but on the other hand, it can be rewarding. In some schools, the materials may be in short supply or non-existent simply because scarce funds are used to meet other instructional needs within the school.

OVERCOME OBSTACLES

One way teachers can overcome these obstacles involves asking parents to donate everyday materials, such as empty toilet paper rolls, nails, paste, buttons, wire, newspapers, paper clips, or similar products. It's best to make this request at the beginning of the school year. However, you can also request specific items at the time you plan to teach a particular lesson. For example, ask parents to donate tin foil and masking tape for an upcoming electricity lesson, or ask for donations of toy cars, paper cups, and small blocks for a lesson on Newton's Laws of Motion.

If you can, distribute a printed list the first day of school, so students can take the list home and bring in the materials in a timely way, assuring you have what you need in time for a lesson. Before teaching a particular lesson, you can also list the teaching tools you need on the whiteboard or the SMART Board, providing students with a daily reminder to bring the materials to the classroom. You can keep these reminders going until you have gathered the majority of your supplies.

PLAN AHEAD AND GATHER MATERIALS

Teachers would be wise to plan ahead and organize a list of needed materials and submit it to their administrators, either at the beginning of or during the school year. Doing this helps teachers gather the necessary tools to develop a hands-on learning experience. Understandably, teachers work in a variety of settings, and some find they have minimal resources available, while others teach in environments where an abundance of funds exist to meet teaching needs. Regardless of circumstances, however, *it never hurts to ask.*

It can also be satisfying to search for materials you need. For example, in some schools, teachers/administrators have bought science kits or science manipulatives and teachers find them stored in various places such as the library, the cafeteria, back stage with theater supplies, in other science rooms, in an out-of-the way closet, or in another teacher's classroom. Try to locate these resources by checking for an inventory list that might have been created and previously distributed to the faculty; or, ask your colleagues if they know where these materials are located. Sometimes word-of-mouth is your best resource. Whatever way your school stores science materials, it's your responsibility to spend the time to locate them. In the long run, the effort is worth it, because your science teaching will be more meaningful and help bridge the gap between learning by rote and learning through understanding.

ESTABLISH A PLACE

Consider the best way to organize your materials before the time comes to present them to your students. Prior to the lesson and before you distribute the materials to your cooperative learning groups (see Step Seven), it's advantageous to arrange them on your desk or on a small table. First, give specific oral or written directions on their use, and then ask the materials managers (see Step Seven) to collect the materials for their cooperative learning group and then return them after their groups have used them.

Teachers find they have more time to observe students during the learning process if they have prepared and organized their materials and provided directions about their use. In an organized learning environment, students are more likely to be ready to tackle the challenge of solving an investigation together. In addition, in an organized environment the progression of learning science becomes more meaningful and more student-centered.

MOTIVATE YOUR STUDENTS

Furthermore, teachers should motivate students' interest by displaying collections of rocks or shells in the classroom, for example, or any other pertinent science models that are relevant to the concept being studied. If living organisms are being investigated, have models of plastic animals available; if force and motion are being investigated, have small play cars and plastic ramps available to manipulate and explore.

Teachers can also set up a Science Corner that coincides with the concept you're teaching that week or that month. This designated area could provide various tools used to conduct investigations, such as timers, magnifying lens, graduated cylinders, flasks, or microscopes; it's beneficial to let your students manipulate and touch them in simple ways.

If you're teaching upper elementary students, have similar materials scattered around the classroom for students to observe and handle before the bell rings for class. Create interactive bulletin boards, such as a weather map that allows students to write the air temperature, barometric pressure, or rainfall for a particular region. Or place small mystery boxes with holes filled with different items for students to feel and guess their contents. Posters, available inexpensively, are another trouble-free method for encouraging science learning. The following internet sites supply free posters:

- http://busyteacher.org/teaching_ideas_and_techniques/classroom-posters/
- http://www.zazzle.com/free+for+teachers+posters
- http://edgalaxy.com/classroom-posters-charts/

KEY POINTS

- It's worth taking the time to assemble materials for teaching science; it can be exasperating but rewarding.
- Use all the resources at your disposal to locate existing materials, ask for donations, or if necessary, use school funding to buy them.
- Advance planning creates an atmosphere in which students are eager to experiment and learn.
- Use your classroom as an interactive science environment, where there is always something appealing to view or use.
- Keep the goal in mind: You want your students to come away with a love for all things science, including the skills that allow them to appreciate the world around them and solve everyday problems.

STEP SEVEN

Establish Cooperative Learning Groups

Science, in the very act of solving problems, creates more of them.

Abraham Flexner[1]

Establishing cooperative learning groups is one of the most effective means for teaching science. Linn & Burbules[2] describe a *cooperative* learning group as one that divides a task into parts, with each member completing one part of the whole project. A *collaborative* learning group has two or more students jointly solving a single solution for a problem. Since my main focus for teaching and learning science is inquiry, which necessitates group learning in an open, guided, or structured approach (see Step Five), you have the option to choose either cooperative or collaborative grouping. For purposes of this guidebook, I'm referring to both types of grouping as cooperative learning.

Researchers have found that five students is the ideal number for interacting, cooperating, and engaging in a learning situation. In many cases, this idea isn't feasible because of the number of students in a class, so teachers must adapt the ideal and group students as best they can. However, I recommend keeping the groups as close to five members each as possible. Of course, it's also beneficial to make individual and whole group instruction part of your overall plan. That said, I believe cooperative groups lead to better communication among students, more interactive hands-on learning, and students taking greater responsibility for their learning.

THE SCIENCE PROCESS SKILLS/PRACTICES

The science process skills or practices as mentioned in the Next Generation Science Standards, basic and integrated, are transferable abilities and scientific skills that mirror the behavior of scientists in the field. These skills encourage students to hypothesize and they also promote critical thinking.[3] In this guidebook, and in general when discussing most primary elementary grades, I tend to emphasize the basic process skills. However, when teaching the intermediate elementary grades, you can also encourage some of the integrated skills, such as controlling variables, formulating hypotheses, interpreting data, experimenting, and creating models, depending on the grade level and the ability of your students.

As students collaborate in their groups, the basic science process skills/practices; observing, measuring, inferring, classifying, predicting, and communicating, become central to "doing" science. "When we teach students to use these skills in science, we are also teaching them skills that they will use in the future in every area of their lives."[4]

Let's assume that we want to create an atmosphere where our students strive to become "mini-scientists." As scientists they have to reach a solution to a problem by asking many questions. During that process, they evaluate the problem at hand by using their five senses, measure and classify it by using mathematical skills, and make inferences and predictions based on prior experiences, not necessarily in any order. Students at different age levels may simply use one skill over another or even combine them. What is important is that students understand the process and can apply the skills to everyday life.

LEARNING COMMUNICATION SKILLS

Communication, one of the science process skills/practices, is a method of expressing and exchanging thoughts and ideas to others. This communication can be verbal, nonverbal, visual, or modeled.[5] Students given opportunities to communicate while working in a cooperative group learn to develop a language of science and converse using scientific terminology and vocabulary. Throughout the process they become adept at creating science discourse, meaning they can explain and discuss scientific phenomenon.

Needless to say, grouping students and giving them opportunities to collaborate leads to better understanding and a more sophisticated grasp of the science concept. Forming collaborative learning groups encourages a continuous circle of peer communication in reaching consensual agreement and optimizes students' experiences. At the same time, collaborative learning allows students to change previous ideas and beliefs and construct new and different understandings.[6–8]

In the scientific world, scientists generally face a problem they must solve. They gather appropriate data and try to solve the problem based on their findings. As a result of reaching a solution, they publish their findings, present papers, and assemble at conferences to share information. These avenues provide scientists an environment in which to exchange their ideas and formulate and construct new thoughts. As teachers, we should provide the same scenarios in our science classrooms by implementing cooperative learning groups, which serve as examples of what scientists do every day, i.e., exploring, experimenting, justifying, evaluating, sharing, and modifying.

ENCOURAGING INTERACTION

Cooperative learning groups also offer students optimum time to interact with their peers in a hands-on learning fashion. When you have a small number of students in a cooperative learning group, the manipulatives become more accessible and that means each student in the group has a chance to touch, maneuver, and operate them. In addition, when fewer students interact, they can maximize their discussion and make the most of their science dialogue. Consequently, students learn to cooperate and take turns, along with helping each other to solve the problem at hand. Teamwork becomes an asset and over time, students come to realize that without it they'd find it difficult to achieve their common goal of reaching a solution. "Children love to interact with their peers by listening and responding to each others' ideas. By collaboratively seeking a solution, they gain respect for each others' viewpoints and learn to interpret a more accurate understanding of scientific knowledge."[9]

Obviously, students take greater responsibility when working in a cooperative learning group because the structure itself demands that each member contribute to the whole group. This also means that students generally aren't isolated, and they also experience less peer competition. If they don't work cooperatively, they soon realize that they can't accomplish the end result, which is reaching a solution to a joint problem.

STRUCTURE OR NON-STRUCTURE

A truly effective form of cooperative learning maintains structure and focus. However, some teachers believe that group learning can result in a non-structured learning environment where students are noisy and appear to be loud and not task-oriented; true teamwork emphasizes an exchange of ideas, which may appear raucous and rowdy, with continuous conversation and with students concentrating on a specific goal.

I have found that assigning a specific job to each student within the group achieves a sound spirit of teamwork and provides each with a sense of responsibility and makes each accountable for their actions. Students tend to concentrate more and appear to be more directed toward the task at hand. For example, possible jobs might include project director, assistant director, materials manager, reporter, and team member. The project director is the "teacher" and makes sure that each student is participating and contributing; the assistant director assists the director; the materials manager is responsible for getting and returning all supplies to the teacher; the reporter records and reports the group's consensus; and the team member organizes and cleans the area.

These jobs could carry various names, but the basic responsibilities remain the same. In my classroom, I supply students with laminated colored nametags to tie around the neck or ones placed on the desk in front of each student, depending on the age group. You could also just color code them for the primary grades with a specific color representing a responsibility. Some teachers use colored clothespins or names of plants to represent each job (see Appendix III). These nametags and job titles add to the sense of belonging to a team.

KEY POINTS

* Cooperative group learning helps students understand scientific collaboration.
* Cooperative learning groups emphasize using the basic science skills or practices that emulate the work of scientists, which prepare them for the real world.

- Cooperative learning groups teach communication and interaction skills, through which students learn, yet maintain their individuality.
- Five is an ideal number for cooperative learning groups.
- Assign specific jobs to each member of a group.
- Encourage focus and commitment toward a mutual purpose by coordinating students' efforts to achieve a common goal.

NOTES

[1] Flexner A. (1930). *Universities* (p. 1). Retrieved from http://www.quotegarden.com/science.html

[2] Linn, M. C., & Burbules, N. C. (1993). Construction of knowledge and group learning. In K. Tobin (Ed.), *The practice of constructivisim in science education* (pp. 91–119). Hillsdale, NJ: Lawrence Erlbaum Associates.

[3] Padilla, M. J. (1990, March 1). *The science process skills* (Research Matters–to the Science Teacher no. 9004). Reston, VA: National Association for Research in Science Teaching (NARST). Retrieved from https://www.narst.org/publications/research/skill.cfm

[4] Longwood University. (2014). *How can we understand our water resources? Teaching the science process skills* (p. 5). Retrieved from http://www.longwood.edu/cleanva/images/sec6.processskills.pdf

[5] Broadview University. (2015). *Skills you need: Communication skills.* Retrieved from http://www.skillsyouneed.com/general/communication-skills.html

[6] Bruffee, K. A. (1993). *Collaborative learning: Higher education, interdependence and the authority of knowledge.* Baltimore, MD: The Johns Hopkins University Press.

[7] Roth, W. M. (1993). Construction sites: Science labs and classrooms. In K. Tobin (Ed.), *The practice of constructivism in science education* (pp. 143–170). Hillsdale, NJ: Lawrence Erlbaum Associates.

[8] Tobin, K. (1993). Preface: Constructivism: A paradigm for the practice of science education. In K. Tobin (Ed.), *The practice of constructivism in science education* (pp. ix–xvi). Hillsdale, NJ: Lawrence Erlbaum Associates.

[9] Greenspan, Y. F. (1998). *Learning science with action experiments, as seen through the eyes of a teacher* (p. 3). Presented at the annual meeting, National Association for Research in Science Teaching, San Diego, CA.

STEP EIGHT

Implement Technology

Any sufficiently advanced technology is indistinguishable from magic.

Arthur C. Clarke

In today's world, new technologies play important roles in day-to-day life in nearly every part of the world. From television and Smart Phones, IPads and personal computers in all shapes and sizes, we're connected by our constantly evolving technology-driven world. Individuals, including many children, use the Internet to access information and social media to interact with each other.

SCIENCE, TECHNOLOGY, ENGINEERING, AND MATHEMATICS – OR STEM

Leading researchers now suggest that teachers integrate a curriculum that includes science, technology, engineering and mathematics, known as STEM, into their science programs (discussed in Chapter Four). Jobs in these fields are expected to increase in the coming years, so students must be prepared to successfully compete for them. However, despite the expected surge in science and engineering jobs, Morella[1] states that many students do not continue their studies in STEM subjects through all four years of high school. According to Morella, close to 60 percent of the nation's students who begin high school interested in science, technology, engineering, and math – or STEM – change their minds by the time they graduate.[1]

TECHNOLOGY IN THE CLASSROOM

Today, teachers have the responsibility to implement some form of technology into our lessons in order to engage our students and keep their attention on tasks we assign. Since our world dictates having these skills in order to compete in the job market of the future, it's our job as teachers to prepare children to be productive citizens. Dutta explains …"computers have revolutionized the way individuals, students and enterprises work, communicate, live, educate and entertain. Computers are now integral to virtually every possible human and non-human activity."[2]

Laptops now are part of the classroom equipment throughout the United States. In several reports and surveys of teachers using laptops in their classrooms, Zucker and other researchers[3–6] cite these highlights:

- Student engagement – Willingness to work, and the quality of the work is greatly improved; increased student motivation, interest and self-directed learning.
- Greater classroom flexibility during instruction– Having laptops in the classroom is much better than having to schedule or wait for time in the school's computer lab.
- Quick feedback to students – Certain learning programs give rapid feedback, especially helpful for struggling students and more student interaction with teachers.
- Access to up-to-date information – "It's like having an interactive textbook that never becomes obsolete," says a teacher in Maine.
- Enhanced professional productivity – Teachers can design and create materials, prepare lesson plans, diagnose student weaknesses, and communicate and collaborate with colleagues, parents, and students.

On the same note, Warschauer[7] concluded that:

Laptops will not make a bad school good, but they will make good schools better. When part of an instructional program promotes critical inquiry, individually assigned laptops with wireless Internet connections are an invaluable tool for helping students develop the information literacy and research skills required for success in the 21st century.

Other studies suggest that "students who use computers in the classroom show at least a modest level of achievement gain over students who do not use computers."[8]

TECHNOLOGY AND SCIENCE

Initiate a program in your school that gives students opportunities to increase their computer skills and learn science at the same time. Allow them to use the computer to journal what they have learned in science, create documents that summarize and illustrate a concept, and demonstrate and graph their results to present to their classmates. In the primary grades, students can design drawings by learning to cut and paste science pictures from the Internet. In the intermediate grades, students can create their own websites and share them with one another. Teach them how to use an Excel spreadsheet or construct a PowerPoint Presentation. These are technology tools they will likely need in their future workplaces.

In school or at home, our students typically participate daily in educational and recreational video games; they communicate and bond through texting on their Smartphones; and access the Internet on computers or phones or iPads to gain information on various topics. On the negative side, many students in your classroom may have Smartphones that they need to hold onto at all times during the school day so that they can communicate instantly with their parents or guardians in case of emergency. Although this may prove to be a challenge for you during the school day, you can turn a negative situation into a positive learning experience by having students access the Internet, research subject matter, and create brief presentations and journal entries with their own phones. Keep in mind that these technologies are tools we can use to motivate, engage, reinforce, as well as extending and promoting fun into the experience of learning science. As tools, they help inform and entertain, and many times these technologies inspire students to think critically. Therefore, within our science lesson plan framework, we should include real-life and animated videos and access to the Internet when introducing a concept and then again when summarizing or wrapping up a concept. You can find tools to produce videos on sites such as:

- BrainPOP, www.brainpop.com
- Brightstorm, www.brightstormeducation.com/
- Discovery Education, https://www.discoveryeducation.com/search/page/k-5/science/-/-/index.cfm

These websites encourage science learning with many types of animated videos, sample problems, interactive games, and visual examples that describe, explain, and illustrate a specific science concept.

Understanding that the computer is a tool for teaching and learning, think about using it in science for word processing to type and edit documents, for example, or as a resource for gathering information and researching various subject matter. Allow students to research the science or common core standards to give them an idea of learning goals designed for them. Let students access the "apps" appropriate for science learning, such as the study of cells. Retrieve "Siri" for science information in areas such as how to plant seeds or understand the differences between kinetic or potential energy. Many of these sites and apps are geared towards students of all ages and foster science classroom learning.

In addition, allow students to practice using computer-aided technology products, which will increase and enhance their skills in design and analysis and serve as an interactive learning tool. Some examples, among many available, include Gizmos, found at www.explorelearning.com, and Superkids, found at www.superkids.com/aweb/pages/reviews/science/, which promote interactive science learning. Many other kinds of software and beneficial computer resources are available that allow students to reach their potential and achieve success. The SMART Board is another engaging and interactive tool that brings many resources directly into the classroom in a whole group setting and helps both teachers and students learn basic science concepts.

Finally, technology allows students to collaborate with students in different states or countries in order to discover how they learn science. They can also discuss similarities and differences in their science curriculum. What better way can we offer our students the chance to connect so easily to those in other cultures?

Our students must be prepared for the technological reality of this century, and current and future economic and cultural conditions demand that we incorporate all forms of technology into our classrooms.

KEY POINTS

- Today's teachers must incorporate STEM subjects in their curricula to prepare students for the jobs and careers of the future.
- Use online computer programs, apps, and other resources to teach students to create presentations and videos.
- Use today's technology to reach out to science students in other states or countries.
- Stay current about easily accessed computer programs and activities to enhance science teaching.

NOTES

[1] Morella, M. (2013, January 31). *Many high schoolers giving up on STEM.* Retrieved from http://www.usnews.com/news/blogs/stem-education

[2] Dutta, P. (2015). *What are the benefits of computers in society?* (p. 1) Retrieved from http://www.ehow.com/about_5376921_computers-helped-workplace.html

[3] Silvernail, D. L. (2004, February). *The impact of Maine's one-to-one laptop program on middle school teachers and students* (pp. 1–54). Gorham, ME: Maine Education Policy Research Institute. Retrieved from http://maine.gov/mlti/articles/research/MLTIPhaseOneEvaluationReport2004.pdf

[4] Silvernail, D. L. (2011, August). *A middle school one-to-one laptop program: The Maine experience* (pp. 1–41). Gorham, ME: Maine Education Policy Research Institute. Retrieved from http://usm.maine.edu/sites/default/files/cepare/6MLTIBrief2011_MEExp.pdf

[5] Zucker, A. A., & McGhee, R. (2005, February). *A study of one-to-one computer use in mathematics and science instruction at the secondary level in Henrico county public schools* (pp. 1–58). Washington, DC: SRI International. Retrieved from http://ateneu.xtec.cat/wikiform/wikiexport/_media/materials/jornades/jt101/bloc1/henrico_finalreport.pdf

[6] Zucker, A. A., & Hug, S. T. (2007, December). *A study of the 1:1 laptop program at the Denver school of science & technology* (pp. 1–86). Denver, CO: Denver School of Science and Technology. Retrieved from http://files.eric.ed.gov/fulltext/ED500425.pdf

[7] Warschauer, M. (2007, November). Information literacy in the laptop classroom. *Teachers College Record, 109,* (p. 2537). Retrieved from http://www.education.uci.edu/person/warschauer_m/docs/infolit.pdf

[8] Johnson, K. A. (2000, June 14). *Do computers in the classroom boost academic achievement?* (p. 1). Washington, DC: The Heritage Foundation. Retrieved from http://www.heritage.org/research/reports/2000/06/do-computers-in-the-classroom-boost-academic-achievement

STEP NINE

Reflect and Assess

Assessment and learning are two sides of the same coin… When students engage in assessments, they should learn from those assessments.[1]

All assessments gather information, make a judgment, or use information for some purpose. Viable assessments are founded on and driven by the science standards, which translate into learning targets or goals. At times, assessing and evaluating inquiry science learning is both difficult and complex.

INQUIRY-LEARNING ASSESSMENTS

Research tells us that inquiry sounds like this:

- *planning investigations for data* is children deciding the selection of questions, tools, schedules for observation, and units of measurement,
- *data collection to evidence* is children observing systematically, measuring accurately, structuring data, and setting standards for quality control,
- *evidence to searching for patterns and building models* is children constructing and defending arguments, presenting evidence, engaging in mathematical modeling, and using physical and computational tools,
- *patterns and models to generate explanations* is the sound of children posing theories, building and reporting conceptual based models, considering alternatives, and generating new productive questions.[2]

Inquiry assessments should encourage student participation in activities relevant to the learning goals. Some assessments may be conducted through rubrics created by the teacher: teacher observation, such as anecdotal notes; observation rubrics or checklists; or with students writing what they have learned by journaling (see Step Four). Other kinds of assessments can be made through teachers' grading, or from high stakes testing provided by either the state or national level or from test-taking strategies that are taught prior to taking these tests.

THREE KINDS OF ASSESSMENT

In science, we assess learning through the process of gathering information or data, best conducted through oral questioning, observing and listening to students, executing performance tasks, and completing different forms of formal testing. The three kinds of assessment are diagnostic, formative, and summative.

First, diagnostic assessment is used to find out what a student knows before you start teaching and is used to gain understanding of the student's knowledge, interests, and abilities.

Second, formative assessment collects data on student learning during the lesson and may be either formal or informal. Formative assessment provides ongoing feedback for teachers about what their students know, thereby allowing teachers to change their teaching accordingly. Formal formative assessment may be accomplished using a written test; informal formative assessment may be teacher-generated observation checklists or student-friendly rubrics, which judge performance-based responses. Whether teachers or students in cooperative learning groups create informal formative assessments, the following examples help assess the learning outcome:

- elicit questioning;
- conduct discussions;
- incorporate graphic organizers from http://www.eduplace.com/graphicorganizer/;
- apply peer or self-assessments;
- lead group presentations.

Finally, summative assessment, a formal type of assessment, occurs after instruction, with the information gathered used to help teachers assign a grade. Examples of summative formal assessment include standardized tests, multiple choice tests, and end-of-unit examinations, which generally focus on accountability and are often done to label, sort, or classify students.

HOW TO ASSESS IN AN INQUIRY-BASED SCIENCE CLASSROOM

How do we evaluate or assess the learner in an inquiry-based science classroom? Do we evaluate students' memorized knowledge or "conceptual understanding as they engage in activities that involve scientific reasoning, inquiry skills, performances and science?" [3] In my opinion, based on the learning objectives of any science lesson, formative assessment strategies are the best means to assess students' conceptual understanding. Equally important, this type of assessment helps teachers to adapt and modify teaching strategies.

In an analysis of 250 studies comparing classrooms where formative assessment was practiced with those in which it was not practiced, evidence indicates that on almost every kind of academic measure, students whose teachers systematically applied formative assessment techniques outperformed similar students who did not receive such treatment. These differences were significant, both statistically and educationally. [4]

Formative assessments are ongoing, and include observations and reviews performed during the learning process. These assessments provide regular feedback that helps the teacher determine whether or not the student understands and is learning the concept. They may even help teachers alter the curriculum to better serve students' learning, and focus on improving student performance and teacher instruction. Throughout formative assessment, teachers should be aware that the cycle includes goals for student learning, such as science content skills, process skill or practices, and attitudes toward science.

The cycle includes the teacher:

- helping students take the next steps toward learning;
- collecting evidence on student's thinking;
- determining the appropriate next steps for students to work on;
- interpreting the evidence of student thinking;
- making a judgment on student's conceptual understanding.[5]

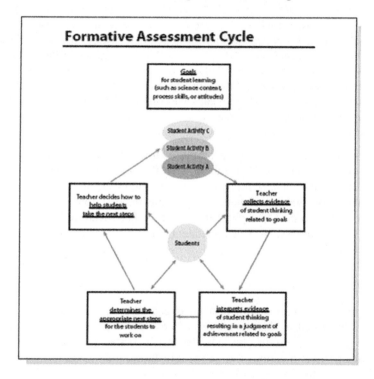

Figure 8. The formative assessment cycle. In the formative assessment cycle, goals are set for student learning. The teacher, acting as a guide, decides how to help students take the next step in comprehending the topic and reaching the designated goals. The teacher collects evidence of student thinking, determines what students should do next, and then interprets how students are thinking so that teaching can be changed or adapted toward a better understanding of the science concept[6]

FORMATIVE ASSESSMENT SAMPLES

The following two samples, a vignette of a lesson on sound and drawings of student work about sound, serve to demonstrate how a teacher would approach assessing students' knowledge, gain feedback, and fittingly adapt the lesson to enhance cognitive understanding of sound.

Vignette One

> In a second grade class, students were investigating and exploring the materials in a sound kit. The teacher required students to raise questions about what they observed and answer those questions by doing their investigations. During their observations, the teacher noticed they used such terms as *pretty high pitched, kind of low pitched, bings,* and *bongs*. The teacher decided they needed to compare pitches of sounds. She modeled a means of recording information in a systematic fashion in hopes they would then develop it on their own. The teacher asked: "Do all four legs of your chair have the same pitch when struck with a pencil?" Demonstrating that there were differences between the sounds of each of the four legs, the back legs were longer than the front legs, the teacher asked why each was different. Students continued their original investigation but the teacher noticed that no group had investigated what affected the volume/loudness of a sound.[7]

The above vignette serves as an example of formative assessment, in which the teacher's task is to gain feedback about what the students learned and then guide them toward a better understanding of what constitutes the notion of volume, pitch, and loudness. Note that the teacher employed only the two front and two back legs to illustrate those concepts.[8] It might have been more beneficial to illustrate the notion of volume, pitch and loudness using students' desks, a file cabinet or even another familiar object in the classroom.

Vignette Two

For a lesson that determines that sound is caused from vibration, primary grade students were asked to draw a picture of how a drum demonstrates sound. The following work from two students indicates that the first student describes how sound occurs, but makes no mention of vibration, and the second student mentions vibration but does not connect it to sound. In the first scenario, the student needs to work on the idea that sound is vibration and in the second, the student needs to consolidate an understanding of how vibration is connected to sound and apply the idea of vibration to this situation. In both cases, the teacher identified what the student does or does not understand; the next step involves suggesting steps to enhance learning, such as having students feel the drumhead when it is hit, describing what happens when it is not hit, or asking if there is a relationship between the sound and the vibration.

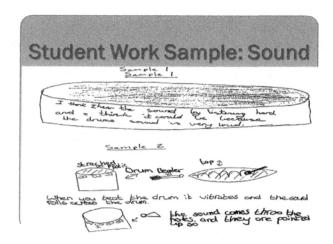

Figure 9. Student work sample on sound. Two students draw pictures of what constitutes sound?

Stiggins suggests "the student's role is to strive to understand what success looks like and to use each assessment to try to understand how to do better the next time."[10] Thus, formative assessments help us differentiate instruction or target instruction to meet individual needs and, as a consequence, improve overall student achievement.

COMMENTING ON STUDENT-WRITTEN WORK

In the above sample drawing, teachers may find the need to provide a written response to the student beyond what has already been given orally, remembering to be positive and non-judgmental. It is important to keep in mind the following:

• Identify one or two aspects for comment and review, which are related to the planned learning goals.
• Comment first (and perhaps only) on aspects specific to science, since the task was set to help learning in science.
• Think carefully about whether or not any other comment is needed at all, such as remarks about neatness or effort, valid though these may be. By all means acknowledge and encourage effort and progress, but not in a way that diverts attention from how to improve and move ahead.
• Pinpoint weak aspects, such as misuse of a technical term, but don't be picky about the use of words or about assertions the student may have made that are not supported by their own evidence.
• Give students time to read, reflect on and, where appropriate, respond to comments.
• Indicate next steps.[11]

REFLECT AND MODIFY

While formative assessments may accomplish learning goals and target student learning, throughout the process of gaining evidence, it's also important that teachers continually reflect on what they have taught, which allows them to better serve the needs of their learning community. With the overall needs in mind, teachers can adjust their lesson, unit of study, or curriculum to help students through conceptual understanding. Teachers can stay mindful of students' previous experiences, prior knowledge, and misconceptions about the concept. Teachers can then ask: "Should I move on?" "Do I need to revisit the instruction to correct any misconceptions or fill in any gaps?"[12]

What should the teacher do during the learning process? Teachers should casually walk around the room, observing how students are learning the science concept, asking quick, short questions, and checking to see if students are using the science process skills/practices. These informal strategies help the teacher to assess and modify future lesson plans and/or units of study. Ultimately, the goal is for students to achieve higher levels of learning and teachers to attain teaching success.

KEY POINTS

- Student learning is routinely assessed using a variety of assessment tools.
- Assessment involves pre-teaching evaluation of students' understanding, as well as post-teaching assessment.
- Formative assessment includes goals for learning, such as science content skills, process skills/practices, and attitudes toward science.
- The advantage of formative assessment is that it allows teachers to observe, question, evaluate, and ultimately modify their teaching to meet students' needs.

NOTES

[1] National Committee on Science Education Standards and National Research Council. (1996). *National science education standards* (p. 1). Washington, DC: National Academy Press. Retrieved from http://www.nap.edu/openbook.php?record_id=4962&page=1

[2] Duschl, R. A. (2011, Summer). The changing landscape of assessment. *Science and Education, 48*(9), 8–9.

[3] Schiller, E., & Melin, J. (2011, Summer). Whoooo knew? *Science and Children, 48*(9), 31.

[4] Black, P. J., & William, D. (1998). Assessment and classroom learning. *Assessment in Education, 1*, 7–74.

[5] Exploratorium Institute for Inquiry. (2006). *Assessing for learning: Workshops designed to introduce teachers to formative assessment* (Workshops I–IV). San Francisco, CA: Exploratorium. Retrieved from www.exploratorium.edu/ifi/workshops/assessing/

[6] Exploratorium Institute for Inquiry. (2006). *Assessing for learning: Workshops designed to introduce teachers to formative assessment* (Workshops I–IV). San Francisco, CA: Exploratorium. Retrieved from www.exploratorium.edu/ifi/workshops/assessing/

[7] Exploratorium Institute for Inquiry. (2006). *Assessing for learning: Workshops designed to introduce teachers to formative assessment* (Workshops I–IV). San Francisco, CA: Exploratorium. Retrieved from www.exploratorium.edu/ifi/workshops/assessing/

[8] Exploratorium Institute for Inquiry. (2006). *Assessing for learning: Workshops designed to introduce teachers to formative assessment* (Workshops I–IV). San Francisco, CA: Exploratorium. Retrieved from www.exploratorium.edu/ifi/workshops/assessing/

[9] Greenspan, Y. F. (2010, Spring). *Assessing science: Ideas for learning* [PowerPoint Slides]. Miami, FL: Miami Dade College.

[10] Stiggins, R. (2007, May). Assessment through the student's eyes. *Educational Leadership, 64*(8), 22. Retrieved from http://www.ascd.org/publications/educational-leadership/may07/vol64/num08/Assessment-Through-the-Student's-Eyes.aspx

[11] Exploratorium Institute for Inquiry. (2006). *Assessing for learning: Workshops designed to introduce teachers to formative assessment* (Workshops I–IV). San Francisco, CA: Exploratorium. Retrieved from www.exploratorium.edu/ifi/workshops/assessing/

[12] Mentor, M. (2008, October). Formative assessments: Real-time responses. *NSTA Reports, 20.*

STEP TEN

Extend and Apply

Ignite curiosity in a young mind and you'll kindle imagination for a life time.[1]

Once a science concept is presented and learners appear interested, it's only natural that their innate curiosity is sharpened to seek more. As a result, the student is stimulated to explore the topic outside the parameters of the lesson.

EXTEND THE LESSON AND APPLY SCIENCE TO EVERYDAY LIFE

A perfect example to expand and extend upon a lesson is a hands-on activity on Isaac Newton's First Law of Motion, the Law of Inertia, which states: An object at rest will remain at rest unless acted on by an unbalanced force and an object in motion continues in motion with the same speed and in the same direction unless acted upon by an unbalanced force.

Students working in their cooperative learning groups can conduct their investigation using toy cars and ramps, discovering why an object at rest will remain at rest unless acted upon by an unbalanced force. At this point, it's the teacher's responsibility to guide students through the process of developing new ideas about motion, by leading a discussion to predict what would happen if there was not an unbalanced force or if the force was balanced.

In addition, to be meaningful to the learner, a scientific concept must be applicable to everyday life. Encourage students to ask questions. How does Newton's First Law of Motion apply to where I live, what I know, and what I want to learn about things in motion? Is it pertinent to driving a car, flying in an airplane, or launching a rocket? Can I observe it in my home? In my school? In my neighborhood? How does it affect what I do every day? These questions (discussed in Step Two) prompt students to think about the way these concepts regularly affect them. The National Capital Language Research Center agrees: "Expansion activities allow students to apply the knowledge they have gained in the classroom to situations outside it. Expansion activities include out-of-class observation assignments, in which the instructor asks students to find examples of something or to use a strategy and report back."[2]

SCIENCE FAIR PROJECTS

Similarly, students can expand on their scientific knowledge and apply it to daily life by creating a science project, easily set up in individual classrooms or as part of a school-wide display. In grades kindergarten, first, and second, science projects may be a team effort, created as a whole class experience and guided by the teacher. Beginning in third grade, students can be encouraged to complete their science projects individually with the help of their teacher and parents. Discovery Education states: "An important part of learning science is doing science. Science fairs offer students an opportunity to practice science investigation and invention. Whether the science fair is competitive or not, the project may be the first time that students choose their own science topic and practice being a scientist or engineer."[3]

As mentioned in Step Five, inquiry-based learning takes many different approaches and serves as a successful method to pursue within the framework of an effective standards-driven science program. One such approach is the scientific method, defined as structured inquiry (see Step Five), and used to create science projects where there is no right or wrong answer. Defined by Garland:

> The scientific method is an ongoing process, which usually begins with observations about the natural world. Human beings are naturally inquisitive, so they often come up with questions about things they see or hear and often develop ideas (hypotheses) about why things are the way they are. The best hypotheses lead to predictions that can be tested in various ways, including making further observations about nature. In general, the strongest tests of hypotheses come from carefully controlled and replicated experiments that gather empirical data. Depending on how well the tests match the predictions, the original hypothesis may require refinement, alteration, expansion or even rejection. If a particular hypothesis becomes very well supported a general theory may be developed.[4]

Creating a science project involves many steps. First, students must be interested in their topics, and teachers can guide students in a direction that holds a special significance for them. Second, teachers must continue to lead students toward accomplishing each step of the scientific method (outlined in Appendix I). Third, the student should conduct the investigation at home, completing each section of the scientific method and recording all data over a sufficient period of time.

Under some circumstances, students are not able to complete the assignment at home so depending on the grade level, teachers should allow daily time slots to complete the task in class. Data should be compiled and presented in either chart or graph form. Then, display all sections on a standard science fair project board, usually sold in local office supply stores, drugstores, or even in local schools at discounted prices (see Appendix I).

Once the investigation and display board are finished, students should present their science project to their peers. The teacher can then create a simple rubric to assess each one (see Appendix I) with the hope that students will feel a sense of pride in achieving success and confidence in science. Everyone should be considered a "winner" for finishing an experiment, thus taking great satisfaction in their accomplishment. Teachers often award their students with a ribbon or other small prize to honor every student who participated in a science fair project.

FIELD TRIPS

In addition, field trips teachers initiate and organize offer a chance for students to increase awareness of the world around them and apply classroom science topics. Although many school budgets and time constraints prevent teachers from planning these fun-filled and educational events, many grant opportunities are available to help teachers expand and enhance their curriculum. For example, you can find grant opportunities through these two foundations:

- http://www.annenbergfoundation.org
- https://www.neafoundation.org/pages/grants-to-educators/

Visiting local indoor or outdoor museums, national parks, or state/county parks allow students to experience concepts and learn first-hand. A field trip is an invaluable tool in gaining a better understanding of science and the world we live in. Students can learn about animals, physics, recycling, local fauna, ecosystems, earth and space, and a plethora of scientific concepts, including STEM related topics simply by being outdoors or by visiting local facilities and museums.[5] According to Jeanpierre: "Museums, even ones without an obvious connection to science, often can offer children hands-on – or even whole body – science experiences in ways individual schools or districts cannot."[6]

Specifically, national and state parks provide a place-based inquiry experience, which offer ideal avenues for learning about ecosystems, habitats, and other concepts that bridge the gap between informal and formal learning communities. The objective is to implement inquiry through STEM with hands-on investigations that integrate mathematics, language arts, and social studies with science. Recently, several national parks and local colleges in the United States teamed up for a joint venture to introduce and model scientific concepts to preservice and inservice teachers. Their curriculum is designed to be adapted for all grade levels in such areas as prescribed fires (fires scheduled by the local national or state parks to preserve an ecosystem); geology, the study of rocks and the process of how those rocks change the Earth's interior and surface; astronomy, the study of the earth's solar system; water's effect on caves; and forest ecology, the study of interrelated patterns and processes of flora and fauna in today's forests. Many interactive activities are designed to move the learner to investigate and gather data to solve a problem based on the evidence collected (see Appendix IV). The following websites may provide further information:

- http://www.nps.gov/acad/planyourvisit/outdooractivities.htm
- http://www.nps.gov/yell/learn/education/classrooms/curriculummaterials.htm
- http://www.nps.gov/teachers/teacher-resources.htm?d=Type:Lesson%2520Plan
- http://www.nps.gov/ever/learn/education/curriculummaterials.htm

EVERYDAY SCIENCE

It goes without saying that in order to increase awareness and understanding of science concepts, students must connect with the lesson. It's the teacher's task to make science applicable to everyday life by asking questions about prior experiences, providing hands-on opportunities, and making it relevant to the students' day-to-day activities. Without that link or connection, students tend to lose interest in the topic and are less motivated to explore it and learn. Students also need to take responsibility for learning by following the steps required to complete an investigation, recording relevant results, and actively participating in real-life encounters. The process of doing science boosts students' self-confidence and sense of purpose as they reach even further to learn and to ask more questions. Only then, does science teaching and learning become a journey for both the educator and the student.

KEY POINTS

- Scientific concepts gain greater meaning when teachers apply them to everyday life.
- Teachers should ask a series of questions that help students observe the way the learned concepts can be observed in students' homes and larger environment.
- Science fairs offer opportunities to exercise the scientific method and gain confidence through experimentation and displaying results.
- Field trips are valuable ways to relate science to everyday life and the surrounding environment; teachers can look for funding through foundations in order to offer this kind of learning opportunity to their students.
- Connecting with scientific concepts through their application to daily life increases awareness and confidence in students.

NOTES

[1]   SRA. (2000). *Teachers make the difference* (p. 56). White Plains, NY: Peter Pauper Press, Inc.
[2]   The National Capital Language Resource Center. (2004). *The essentials of language teaching: Planning a lesson* (p. 1). Retrieved from http://www.nclrc.org/essentials/planning/structure.htm
[3]   Discovery Education. (2011). *Step 1: Getting started* (p. 1). Retrieved from http://school.discoveryeducation.com/sciencefaircentral/Getting-Started.html
[4]   Garland, T. Jr. (2015, March 20). *The scientific method as an ongoing process* (p. 11). Irvine, CA: University of California. Retrieved from http://idea.ucr.edu/documents/flash/scientific_method/story.html
[5]   NSTA Reports. (2014, April). Museums offer hands-on STEM opportunities. *NSTA Reports: National Science Teachers Association, 25*(8), 1–4.
[6]   Jeanpierrre, B. (2014, January). Inquiry in the urban science classroom: Connecting curiosity and creativity. *NSTA Reports, 25*(5), 3.

PART II

LESSON PLANS

INTRODUCTION

In this section, I'm offering some ideas about how to teach an effective science lesson, following the 5E Model for inquiry learning. Aligned with the Next Generation Science Standards, these lessons essentially meet the goals of those standards. I have gathered these lessons over many years of teaching science to elementary students, and I have taught them all in my classroom. Some have been adapted from another source and altered to meet both the needs of my students and to fit my teaching style. *Please feel free to adapt them to suit your needs in your classroom.*

Divided into four disciplinary core ideas: physical sciences; life sciences; earth and space sciences; and engineering, technology, and applications of science, the lessons are separated by grade level – primary and intermediate. I've also included background information and materials needed to teach each science concept, possible home learning assignments, adaptations for your ESE (Exceptional Student Education) learners, the way the concept is connected to other subjects, and examples of real world applications. For the ESL (English as a Second Language) learners, the lessons are hands-on and designed to accommodate to these students' needs. In many cases, you'll note less focus on speaking skills, and more attention given to manipulating the tools to promote understanding a science concept.

I have also included a few of my favorite lessons, because I've found they are highly motivating and attention-grabbing; most tend to fall under the category of physical science, and these lessons also can be modified to use for all grade levels.

In most instances, I've provided handouts you are free to reprint and use with students in your classrooms. I've found that these handouts help students better understand the science concept during the learning process – and that's the goal all teachers share.

PHYSICAL SCIENCES

PS2 – Matter and Stability: Forces and Interactions

PRIMARY LESSON PLAN: MOVING CARS

Background Information

Newton's First Law of Motion: Every object in a state of uniform motion tends to remain in that state of motion unless an external force is applied to it. Push and pull are forces; they make an object move or stop moving. When we push something, we are moving it away from us. When we pull something, we are moving it closer to us.

Materials

Ramps made out of cardboard, books, blocks, different toy cars, masking tape, *Force and Motion with Cars* handout (see below).

Engage

Teacher draws a Spider Map graphic organizer on the whiteboard; one with the word Push, the other with Pull. Brainstorm with students about the concepts of push and pull. Let them describe push? Then, let them describe pull. Compare both, and then the teacher asks if they can think of an example for each. Teacher fills in the 'legs' of the spider with students' responses.

Teacher then reads the book *Motion: Push and Pull: Fast and Slow* by Darlene R. Stille, which discusses how trains and cars move and what may slow them down. Teacher asks students to predict what will happen when a plastic car moves down a ramp (books) after it is pushed a little, or a lot. Teacher demonstrates and writes responses on the whiteboard as students compare the differences in the length the car traveled. Teacher explains that they are going to investigate how a plastic car moves when it is pushed a little and a lot or when there is no push at all.

Explore

Teacher divides students into partner-pairs and gives them each a plastic car, a ramp, and masking tape. Students place masking tape at the bottom of the ramp.

- First, they push the car with one finger,
- Second, they push the car with three fingers,
- Third, they do not push the car, and
- Fourth, they push the car slightly with their hand.

With each step, they measure the distance the car stopped from the bottom of the ramp to the point at which the car stopped, placing a piece of masking tape that indicates where the car stopped each time. Each pair completes the handout (see below).

Explain

Teacher asks:

- What happened to the car when you pushed it with one finger?
- What happened to the car when you pushed it with three fingers?
- With no push?
- With a slight push with your hand?

Students explain results of the handout. Teacher asks students to think of a word that would describe each: far, farther, or farthest.

Elaborate

Teacher asks students if they can think of another example of pushing and pulling. Then, they go on a classroom scavenger hunt, finding things that can push or pull. Teacher leads them in a discussion on pushing a table, or pulling a sled, or a tow truck pulling a stalled car. Teacher asks what would happen if they used a different size car. Would that go further? Why?

Evaluate

Each pair reports on their findings, referring to the handout; they then play game Piggy Push from Cool Math Games http://www.coolmath-games.com/0-piggy-push and/or Hook the Fish from Cookie http://www.cookie.com/kids/games/hook-the-fish.html

Home Learning

Students find objects in their home that they can push or pull and report the next day to their peers.

Adaptations (For Exceptional Student Education)

Set up small cans and use a ball to knock them over.

Possible Connections to Other Disciplines

Integrates STEM and language arts.

Real World Connections

Students should be aware of how this concept affects our daily life, from opening and closing doors to riding in cars and buses, to walking on slippery floors and moving heavy objects.[1]

Force and Motion with Cars

Name_____

Place the words far, farther, and farthest in the correct row.

No Push	
Smaller Push (One finger)	
Small Push (Three fingers)	
Big Push (hand)	

Figure 10. Newton's First Law of Motion: Student handout for collecting data[2]

INTERMEDIATE LESSON PLAN: SMALL MARBLE/LARGE MARBLE

Background Information

Newton's Second Law of Motion: The acceleration of an object as produced by a net force is directly proportional to the magnitude of the net force, in the same direction as the net force, and inversely proportional to the mass of the object.

An object's acceleration depends on the size and direction of the force acting on it and on the mass of the object. A larger force causes more acceleration than a smaller force. A force has more effect on an object with less mass than it has on an object with more mass. Friction is a force that acts against motion when two surfaces rub against each other. Gravity is an invisible force of attraction that makes everything fall down to earth and holds all objects on earth.

Materials

Two grooved metric rulers, one tiny marble, one small marble, one large marble, one washer, one meter tape for measuring, one small paper cup (cut in half lengthwise), masking tape, books, and *Marbles* handout, overhead projector or LCD projector.

Engage

Teacher gives one student a ball to drop from a certain height and asks what happens and why the ball falls. Then the teacher tells all the students to rub their hands together and asks what happens and why. Students should describe both gravity and friction and give other examples of both.

Explore

Teacher divides class into collaborative learning groups of five or six students each, assigning roles such as project manager, assistant manager, materials manager, reporter, recorder, and team manager, (combining the reporter/recorder into one role, depending on your class size). Students may also select their jobs with the consensus of their peers in the group. Students discuss the responsibilities of each job.

Students assemble a ramp with the grooved ruler and several books, placing the half cup with the open end covering the bottom of the ruler. A washer is taped to the top of the cup to add mass. Before beginning the investigation, students are asked to write down their prediction of what they think will happen to the cup when a tiny/small marble and/or a large marble travel down the ramp. Using masking tape to mark the distance, students allow the tiny marble to travel to the cup and label the masking tape T1 for the first trial of the distance of the cup, T2 for the second trial, T3 for the third trial. Students complete the three trials for the tiny marble, and follow the same procedure for the three trials for the small marble (S1, S2, S3) and larger marble (L1, L2, L3), recording data on the sample handout (reproduced below) of how far the cup travels each time.

Explain

Students explain the results of their findings in the completed handout.

Elaborate

Students are asked to think about what would happen if the washer was removed, if another larger marble was used, or to think about other variables that might cause different results.

Evaluate

Teacher recreates the same table either on the whiteboard or an overhead projector or on an LCD projector and records average amounts only from each groups' handout. Students are asked to discuss the combined results and explain and compare differences and similarities.

Home Learning

Students create a poster or home movie on Newton's Second Law of Motion.

Adaptations (For Exceptional Student Education)

Students place wax paper on their ramps and observe what happens to the tiny/small/ large marble. Then they place sand paper on the ramp and observe, discussing their results.

Possible Connections to Other Disciplines

Integrates STEM and language arts.

Real World Connections

Students should be aware that it is easier for two people to push a car than a truck, for example. They should understand why engineers create optimal curves on a bridge and be aware of what happens when they throw or otherwise move a ball in their various sports, such as baseball, basketball, football, and soccer. Students should also think about why it is possible for one person to lift a light box but many people are needed to lift a heavier box.[3]

Marbles

Trials	Tiny Marble	Small Marble	Large Marble
1	cm	cm	cm
2	cm	cm	cm
3	cm	cm	cm
Total	cm	cm	cm
Average	cm	cm	cm

Figure 11. Newton's Second Law of Motion: Student handout for collecting data[4]

NOTES

[1] Lesson Adapted from Miami Dade County Public Schools, Division of Mathematics and Science. (2015). *Resource guides, K-2.* Retrieved from http://science.dadeschools.net/elem/rgk-2ngsss.html

[2] Miami Dade County Public Schools, Division of Mathematics and Science. (2015). *Resource guides, K-2.* Retrieved from http://science.dadeschools.net/elem/rgk-2ngsss.html

[3] Lesson Adapted from Miami Dade County Public Schools, Division of Mathematics and Science. (2015). *Resource guides grade, 3–5.* Retrieved from http://science.dadeschools.net/elem/rg3-5ngsss.html

[4] Miami Dade County Public Schools, Division of Mathematics and Science. (2015). *Resource guides grade, 3–5.* Retrieved from http://science.dadeschools.net/elem/rg3-5ngsss.html

LIFE SCIENCES

LS2 – Ecosystems: Interactions, Energy and Dynamics

PRIMARY LESSON PLAN: FOOD PYRAMID

Background Information

The source of all energy is the sun. The energy from the sun is transferred to plants and then to animals. All plants get their energy from the sun; the plant eaters get their energy from the plants; the meat eaters get their energy from the plant eaters.

Materials

One yellow hat, 12 green plant headbands, six brown plant eater headbands, two red meat eater headbands, bag of popcorn, colored construction paper for hat and headbands.

Engage

Draw a K-W-L chart on the whiteboard and ask the students what they know about the sun. Write their responses in the column labeled K, and then ask the students what they want to know about the sun and write their responses in the column labeled W. Lead them in a discussion with the following questions:

- What comes from the sun? Why?
- How do you know?
- What does the sun do for plants? For animals?
- Why?
- How do you know?

Teacher explains that today students are going to pretend they are the sun, plants, and animals and are going to make a Food Pyramid, asking them if they know what a Food Pyramid is, but not explaining the concept until after the activity.

Explore

- First, teacher selects 12 students to represent the plants and gives them each a green headband that they must wear. They must also sit or kneel in a row side by side.

69

- Next, the teacher selects six students to represent the plant eaters. Each get a brown headband and sits side-by-side in a row behind the plant students.
- Two students are selected to represent the meat eaters and must wear a red headband and sit next to each other behind the plant eaters.
- One child, the sun, is selected to wear a yellow hat and sits in the front of the row of the "plant" students.

The sun is given a bag of popcorn, and each student wearing a green headband takes one handful of popcorn from the sun. Then each person wearing a brown headband takes half of the popcorn from two of the students wearing the green headband, and finally, each person wearing a red headband takes half the popcorn from the three plant eaters.

Explain

Students then try and explain what they observe:

- Where is the sun and why?
- What is the job of the sun?
- How do the plants live?
- How do the plant eaters live?
- How do the meat eaters live?
- Who gets energy directly from the sun?
- What is the job of the plant eaters?
- Who gets all their energy?
- Who do they pass their energy to?

Elaborate

- Why do the meat eaters need energy from more than one plant eater?
- What would happen if the sun was not in the sky?
- What would happen to the plants and the animals?
- What would happen to you?

Evaluate

Students eat their popcorn as teacher completes the L of the K-W-L Chart, asking them what they learned. Students then draw a picture of a Food Pyramid, using our activity as an example.

Home Learning

Students draw the Food Pyramid.

Adaptations (For Exceptional Student Education)

Give students different colors of yarn: yellow, green, brown, red, and have them connect the yarn to pictures of the sun, the plants, the plant eaters, and the meat eaters.

Possible Connections to Other Disciplines

Integrates mathematics, science, language arts, art.

Real World Connections

Students should be aware of the foods they choose in order to understand where they receive the most nutrients, an important source of energy that helps them do the things they want to do.[1]

INTERMEDIATE LESSON PLAN: ANIMAL ADAPTATION

Background Information

Every organism has to adapt to its environment to compete for resources. Birds' beaks are examples of structural adaptations.

Materials

One tablecloth; one-half cup each of: beans, rice, macaroni, Gummy Worms, cooked spaghetti, cooked rice; six each of spoons, clothespins, toothpicks, chopsticks, small fishnets; two paper cups per student; pan of water.

Engage

Teacher shows pictures of different kinds of birds and asks:

- What do you observe about each bird?
- Describe their body parts.
- How are they different from a dog?
- From a cat?

Now let's just talk about their faces:

- What do you observe?
- Why do you think their beaks are different?

Discussion will continue until students agree that animals adapt to their environment; specifically, birds have different types of beaks to help them survive.

Explore

Teacher divides students into cooperative learning groups of five or six in each group, Roles can be assigned or students may select their own roles with the consensus of the group project manager, assistant manager, materials manager, reporter/recorder, and team manager (combining the reporter/recorder into one role, depending on your class size. Discuss responsibilities of each job.

Students sit with their group at a table covered with a tablecloth and a variety of food that birds might eat, such as macaroni, beans, gummy worms, cooked spaghetti, and rice. Each student receives one tool to represent a beak, i.e., toothpick, clothespin, chopstick, spoon, small fishing net and an empty paper cup. Also, each group receives a pan of water with the same foods to represent what water birds eat. Students have several minutes to catch the food they want to eat using their tool, and then placing their catch in the empty cup or the water cup.

Explain

Students examine the food they caught and explain what tool was used and why it was significant to catching that food. Teacher asks how this is relevant to birds and how different adaptations allow each type of beak to catch a certain food. Teacher further asks students to think about what possible type of bird each simulated beak represented and how its beak (adaptation) enabled the bird to eat the different types of food.

Elaborate

Students research the actual type of bird each simulated beak represented and how this adaptation enabled the bird to eat each kind of food. Then each group selects another animal and describes a new adaptation that would help it survive.

Evaluate

Students write a group or individual report about the relationship between the bird-beak adaptation and the food they are able to consume.

Home Learning

Students write a brief report on other adaptations not discussed in class, such as camouflage. Students, who have computers, may access BrainPop at the following website:

> https://www.brainpop.com/science/ecologyandbehavior/camouflage/
> preview.weml

Adaptations (For Exceptional Student Education)

Students conduct the same experiment but only use spoon and toothpicks.

Possible Connections to Other Disciplines

Integrates science, technology, social studies, and language arts.

Real World Connections

Students should think about the way they adapt to their environment such as a change in weather, when it's cold or very hot, for example, and how changing conditions influence what they wear and what they do.[2]

NOTES

[1] Lesson Adapted from Lingelbach, J. (n.d.). *Hands-on nature. Center for excellence.* Miami, FL: Museum of Science, Inc.

[2] Lesson Adapted from Miami Dade County Public Schools, Division of Mathematics and Science. (2015). *Resource guides grade, 3–5.* Retrieved from http://science.dadeschools.net/elem/rg3-5ngsss.html

EARTH AND SPACE SCIENCES

ESS1 – Earth's Place in the Universe

PRIMARY LESSON PLAN: LEARNING ABOUT THE WATER CYCLE

Background Information

The water cycle is a continuous movement of water on the earth's surface and below it. Water can move from one reservoir to another, from a river to an ocean, or from an ocean to the atmosphere. This is accomplished through the physical processes of:

- evaporation (water turning into vapor or gas);
- condensation (water turning from vapor or gas into liquid water);
- precipitation (water released from clouds in the form of rain, freezing rain, sleet, snow or hail);
- transpiration (water transported through the roots of plants to the spores under the leaves and changes to vapor; i.e., evaporation of water in plant leaves).

When water evaporates it cools the atmosphere and when it condenses, it warms the atmosphere, and that leads to temperature change and influences on climate.

Materials

One pint size zip-lock bag, masking tape, magnifying lens, water, beads of various colors, yarn or leather straps.

Engage

Teacher and students draw a picture of the Water Cycle on the whiteboard or on paper, similar to the examples below. Discuss evaporation, condensation, precipitation, and transpiration and the water cycle.

Explore

Divide the class into collaborative learning groups of five or six students each. Assign roles such as project manager, assistant manager, materials manager, reporter/recorder, and team manager (combining the reporter/recorder into one role, depending on your class size). Discuss responsibilities of each job. Pass out one

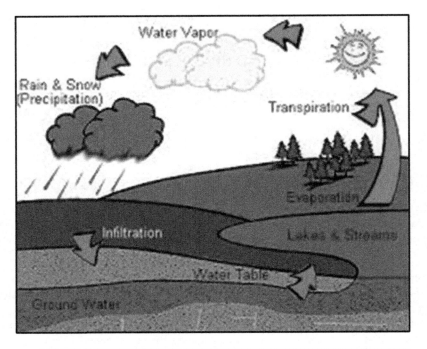

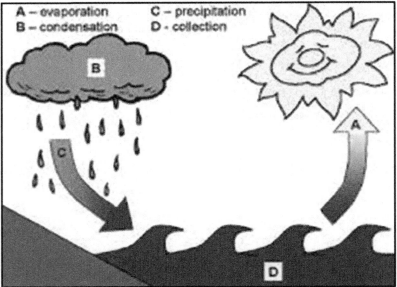

Figure 12. Example of water cycle drawings[1]

baggie and one magnifying lens to each group. Place approximately two ounces of water in the baggie and mark the water line. Close the baggie tightly, tape it, and put it in a warm place, preferably on a window where there is direct sun. The objective is to learn what happens to liquid water when it evaporates in a closed system. Observe for five to ten days.

Explain

Students create a graph (see below) and graph their observations over a period of ten days. Each group explains their observation, using the graph as their visual aide and explaining why their results either differ or are similar to other groups.

Elaborate

Students may perform the same experiment with modifications listed below and observe for another ten days, followed by graphing and explaining their results:

• Salt water instead of plain water, being an example of desalination.
• Different liquids such as milk, Sprite, apple juice, Gatorade.
• Different amounts of light, color of baggie, amount of water and/or sizeof baggie.

Evaluate

Teacher collects graphs and students create a water cycle bracelet (see below).

Home Learning

Students wear bracelets home and have to explain to their families what each bead represents and how it is relevant to the water cycle.

Adaptations (For Exceptional Student Education)

Students use a large baggie for observation.

Possible Connections to Other Disciplines

Integrates mathematics, science, language arts, art.

Real World Connections

Students should be aware that water has an impact on us every day, from the water we and other animals need to ingest in order to survive, to washing our clothes, our dishes, and our bodies, to swimming and making our plants grow.[2]

Water Evaporation (Title)

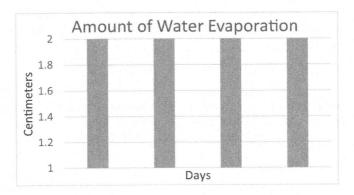

Figure 13. Water evaporation graph[3]

The Water Cycle Bracelet

Materials: Beads of various colors (yellow, clear, green, white, blue), leather straps or yarn

Color of Bead	Represents
Yellow	Sun
Clear	Evaporation
Green	Transpiration
White	Clouds/Condensation
Blue	Precipitation [4]

INTERMEDIATE LESSON PLAN: WEATHER STATION

Background Information

Weather is constantly changing, and is a condition of the outside air at any time or place. Changes in weather patterns determine whether we walk to school, drive a car, or take a bus. It determines what we wear to school and how we feel. Climate, however, is the big picture and is defined as weather over a long period of time.

Both weather and climate affect our daily lives, from what we wear to the crops we grow, to the design of our homes, and even to our physical health and mental well-being. The cause and effect of climate has increased our awareness of the greenhouse effect, which occurs when the Earth's atmosphere traps solar radiation because of the presence of certain gases, resulting in warmer air temperatures and global warming. Global warming is a descriptive term for long term changes. It refers to a gradual increase in the average temperature of the Earth's atmosphere and its oceans, whereas climate change refers to changes in global climate, such as precipitation patterns and extreme weather patterns, such as drought and heat waves.

Materials

Use the following weather instruments:

- thermometer (measures the air temperature);
- barometer (measures the atmospheric pressure);
- anemometer (measures wind speed);
- wind vane (measure wind direction);
- rain gauge (measures the amount of rain);
- hygrometer (measures amount of humidity).

You also need photographs of different kinds of clouds, graph paper, drawing paper, small notebooks, and *My Group Work* handout. (see below for designs to create weather instruments).

Engage

Teacher creates a mystery box and places statements about evaporation, condensation, temperature, precipitation, the greenhouse effect, and global warming in it. Each student selects one statement and responds to it.

Explore

Teacher divides class into collaborative learning groups of five to six students each, assigning roles such as project manager, assistant manager, materials manager, reporter/recorder, (combining the reporter/recorder into one role, depending on your class size), and team manager. Students may also select their jobs with the consensus of their peers in the group. Students discuss the responsibilities of each job. One student in the class will serve as the weather reporter. Each group records daily temperature, barometric pressure, humidity, cloud formations, wind direction and velocity, and rainfall; they observe weekly and monthly weather patterns. This can be accomplished before the first bell rings, during the school day, or shortly after the dismissal bell.

Explain

Data are collected and graphed and shared among group members and communicated with the whole class every three days. Data are also given daily to the weather reporter, who may share results with entire school through daily announcements or regularly with the whole class.

Elaborate

Students track precipitation and air temperature patterns for their local community over the past five years. Then they find the elevation of three major coastal cities in the United States, including their local city if it's in a coastal locale, and compare their precipitation and air temperature patterns. Students write journal entries about the way each would be affected by a rise in ocean level of ten feet.

Evaluate

Teacher observes students as they work in groups collecting data. Data are recorded monthly on a graph and assessed for accuracy and creativity. Teacher collects completed *My Group Work Evaluation* handout.

Home Learning

Students observe cloud formations daily for two weeks and report their findings to class.

Adaptations (For Exceptional Student Education)

Students report daily findings through drawings on an in-house television morning news or within the classroom.

Possible Connections to Other Disciplines

Integrates STEM, language arts, social studies, and art.

Real World Connections

Students should be aware that weather influences what we wear, what we drink, what we eat, how much sun we need or don't need, and how weather makes life possible on Earth.

Designing Your Own Weather Instruments

Thermometer

Tap water, rubbing alcohol (*remind students not to drink this*), clear, narrow-necked plastic bottle (11-ounce water bottles if possible), food coloring, clear plastic drinking straw, modeling clay.

- Pour equal parts of tap water and rubbing alcohol into the bottle, filling about one-eighth to a one-fourth of the bottle.
- Add a couple of drops of food coloring and mix.
- Put the straw in the bottle, making sure the straw does not touch the bottom (*remind students not to drink mixture*).
- Use the modeling clay to seal the neck of the bottle, so the straw stays in place.
- Now hold your hands on the bottle and watch what happens to the mixture in the bottle.[5]

Or refer to the following video on how to make a thermometer for Grades 1–3 http://www.ehow.com/video_12295222_teach-first-graders-thermometers.html

Anemometer

Five paper cups, two straws, pencil with eraser, glue, single-hole punch.

- Mark where you want to poke your holes in each paper cup and then poke holes through each one. Make the holes so that you can put a straw through two cups so line it up properly. Do the same thing to the other pair of cups.
- Poke a pencil through the fifth cup in the center. Line it up straight and poke it through from the bottom of the cup.
- Make the cups stay on the straws by using glue that sticks quickly or sturdy masking tape.[6]

Figure 14. Example of anemometer[7]

Wind Vane

Round plastic drinking cup with lid, such as a yogurt cup, or a round food storage container with lid, paper plate, pebbles or sand, modeling clay, sharpened pencil, drinking straw (a straight one), straight pin, poster board or card stock paper, black permanent marker, compass, ruler, glue.

Figure 15. Example of wind vane[8]

- Put the lid on the plastic container, and turn the container upside down. Trace around the lid, and then using a paper plate, make another circle around the outer edge, at least two inches wider than the first one.
- With a ruler, divide the paper plate in half along its diameter, and then divide each of those halves in half. Write the words for the four parts of the compass along the outer edge of each of the four sides: north, east, south, and west.
- Open the container. Place a blob of modeling clay or putty on the bottom of the container, and then fill the remainder to the top with pebbles or sand. Snap the container lid on and tape it, if necessary, to keep it secure.
- Glue the container, upside down onto the cardboard compass base (paper plate) you just made.
- Take the sharpened pencil and poke it through the center of the plastic container so that the eraser is on top, and the point is held by the putty and sand.
- Cut a broad triangle and a square, both about three inches across from your construction paper. Cut a slit in each end of the straw. Slide the triangle onto one end and the square onto the other. Use a bit of glue if necessary. Push the pin through the center of the straw and attach it to the top of the pencil.
- Go outside to a place where the wind is not highly obstructed. Using the compass, find north, south, east, and west, and line up the wind vane accordingly. Wait for a breeze.[9]

Rain Gauge

Two liter plastic bottle, scissors, duct tape, sand, marker, ruler.

Figure 16. Example of rain gauge[11]

- Empty and wash out the two liter bottle.
- With the scissors, cut off the spout top right where the taper or curve begins.
- Fill bottom of the bottle with one half inch of sand. This will keep the bottle from falling over.
- Pour in just enough water so you can see the water level above the sand, the saturation point.

- Use the marker to draw a line at the saturation point above the sand. Next to the line write "starting point."
- Line the ruler up (from the starting/saturation point) and draw a line for every inch up to the top of the bottle. Go back and use the marker to add dots for one-fourth, one half, three-fourths inch spots between every inch.
- Take the top "cut off" spout portion of the bottle and flip it upside down. Insert it into the bottle and use some duct tape to secure it. This part will help catch and collect the rainfall by funneling into your bottle.
- Find a good place to put your rain gauge. Make sure nothing is blocking it from above and it's in a stable wide open area.[10]

My Group Work

Date_____Activity_____

Assessment Category	Excellent	Good	Fair	Poor
Did the group work well together?				
Did everyone in the group have a chance to brainstorm?				
Did everyone in the group participate together?				
Did every one follow their role assignment?				
Did you use the required materials correctly?				
Did you have enough time to complete the activity?				
Overall, how well do you think your group did?				

What did you like best?_____

What did you have difficulty with?_____

_____

Signature of group members:

_____

Figure 17. My group evaluation handout[12]

NOTES

[1] Diagrams of Water Cycle. Retrieved from https://www.google.com/search?q=water+cycle+drawing s&biw=1280&bih=595&tbm=isch&tbo=u&source=univ&sa=X&ved=0CDEQ7AlqFQoTCPndjonJj 8gCFYSUDQodOukOLg

[2] Lesson adapted from Teaching the Water Cycle. (2015). *7 Ideas to teach the water cycle*. Retrieved from https://www.pinterest.com/pin/57843176440268585/

[3] You should always review the attributes of a graph; title, x Axis (horizontal) and y Axis (vertical) and how to calculate what numbers to use. You should also indicate if you want your students to create a bar, line or picture graph.

[4] Water Cycle Bracelet Handout adapted from a lesson created by Stella Stetsky. (n.d.).

[5] Science projects. (2006). *Make a thermometer*. Retrieved from http://www.energyquest.ca.gov/ projects/thermometer.html

[6] Wikihow: To Do Anything. (2015). *How to make an anemometer*. Retrieved from http://www.wikihow.com/Make-an-Anemometer

[7] Example of an Anemometer Retrieved from http://www.wikihow.com/Make-an-Anemometer

[8] Example of a Wind Zane. Retrieved from http://www.education.com/activity/wind+vane/

[9] Education.com. (2015). *How to make a wind vane*. Retrieved from http://www.education.com/ activity/article/wind_vane_first/

[10] Weird Science Kids. (2015). *Process to make a rain gauge*. Retrieved from http://www.weirdsciencekids.com/RainGauge.html

[11] Example of a Rain Gauge. Retrieved from http://www.weirdsciencekids.com/RainGauge.html

[12] Adapted from Miami-Dade County Public Schools, Division of Mathematics and Science Education. (1997). *Sci-TV, Fifth Grade*. Miami, FL.

ENGINEERING, TECHNOLOGY, AND APPLICATIONS OF SCIENCE

ETS1 – Engineering Design

PRIMARY LESSON PLAN: BOAT BUILDING

Background Information

Buoyancy is the upward push or force of water. The shape of an object affects the amount of water that it pushes out of the way or displaces. When the amount of water has greater mass than an object, that object will float (stays on the surface of the liquid). If the displaced water has less mass than the object, the object will sink (does not stay on the surface of the liquid). A large ship floats because its mass is less than the amount of water it displaces.

Materials

Wood block, piece of plastic, washer, toy duck, rubber ball, 30 pennies, balance scale, three pieces of clay (each about 50g), small container filled with water.

Engage

Teacher shows students pictures of small boats and large ships, asking:

- What do you see?
- Tell me about the boat/ship?
- What is it doing?
- Does the boat/ship sink or float?
- Describe a boat/ship that sinks.
- Describe a boat/ship that floats.
- How do you think the boat/ship in the picture floats?

The teacher tells students that the class is going to have a boat building challenge to see which boat (clay) they create holds the most passengers (pennies).

Explore

Divide the class into partner-pairs. Give each partner-pair a small container of water with a block of wood, piece of plastic, and washers. Ask them to predict what will happen to each object: Will it sink or float? Teacher writes results on the whiteboard.

Students remove objects from their small container and receive a piece of clay to construct their own boat. Each pair creates their own boat, first predicting, and then testing it in the small container of water to see how many passengers (pennies) it will hold until it sinks.

Explain

Each partner-pair will share and show their boat design to the class and tell how many passengers it was able to hold. After all have been shared, the teacher will ask students to compare different/similar boats and explain why some held more passengers than others.

Elaborate

Students could use aluminum foil or half paper cups to build their boats; paper clips or marbles could replace the pennies. Then they share, compare, and discuss.

Evaluate

Students draw pictures of their boats in their science journals and, if possible and depending on the grade level and students' ability, explain their results.

Home Learning

Students create a simple chart that reviews what objects sank and what objects floated; they may draw and/or label objects.

Adaptations (For Exceptional Student Education)

Students read *What Floats? What Sinks?* by J. Boothroyd. Students use film canisters or small plastic containers filled with various amounts of water, testing different objects, and observing what floats and what sinks.

Possible Connections to Other Disciplines

Integrates STEM, language arts, and art.

Real World Connections

Students should be aware of how important buoyancy is to boats, submarines, ships, scuba divers, and swimmers in fresh water and ocean water (i.e., that it is not necessary to kick our feet or swirl our arms that much when swimming in the sea).[1]

INTERMEDIATE LESSON PLAN: BUILDING BRIDGES

Background Information

In architecture, a column is the upright, cylindrical, load-bearing part that stands free of the walls and supports the roof of a building or an entablature, the superstructure of moldings and bands, which lie horizontally above the columns. Unlike a pillar, which can be square, oval, or rectangular, a column is always round. The three types of columns in classical Greek architecture are Doric, Ionic, and Corinthian and a colonnade is a row of any of these columns.

Materials

Large piece of wood, books, *My Bridge Design Proposal* (handout), 50 sheets of 8.5 × 11 letter paper (six for each group), scotch tape, colored paper nametags designating title and job description of architect, engineer and contractor (see below), a balance scale with gram unit cubes and Bridge Data Handout.

Engage

Teacher sets up a "bridge" consisting of a large piece of wood balanced on two books on each side and two in the middle. A student is selected to "walk across the bridge." Teacher asks what is needed to cross a bridge (motion and balance) and ask students to research on http://moodleshare.org/course/view.php?id=120 to find different kinds of bridges. After ten minutes, students share what they learned.

Explore

Students are placed in groups of three. Students decide who receives the job title of *architect* (brainstorms design with peers, designs columns, gathers materials, adds data to class chart (*Bridge Data Handout*), *engineer* (gathers materials, builds the structure), *contractor* (selects sizes of books, weighs books used, records the number of books used on bridge, calculates the weight of the total of books). Students make nametags of their job title. Each group completes the handout below *My Bridge Design Proposal*, deciding among themselves which bridge would be the best to support the most weight. Bridges are designed and tested, using one book at a time.

Explain

Students share their designs, explaining why their design was able to hold the amount of weight.

Elaborate

Students may use other objects, such as lighter weight books to test column design or construct bridge out of clay, straws, or Popsicle sticks with glue. Then they share and compare their new results.

Evaluate

Teacher collects and assesses *My Bridge Design Proposal* and completed *Bridge Data Handout* to be displayed on LCD or overhead projector.

Home Learning

Students design a bridge from straws (distributed by the teacher) and share with peers.

Adaptations (For Exceptional Student Education)

Students change height or width of the paper, change paper to construction paper, cardboard, newspaper or clay, and/or change scotch tape to masking tape.

Possible Connections to Other Disciplines

Integrates STEM, language arts, social studies, and art.

Real World Connections

Students should be aware that bridges support cars and trucks of all sizes and that there are many different kinds of bridges, such as *beam bridges, arch bridges, truss bridges* and *suspension bridges*. All of these bridges are spread over long distances based on their dimensions down to the lengths they can cross in a single span, which is the distance between two bridge supports. We can see them on roads, streets and highways all across our cities and towns. Without them, it would be difficult to travel from one place to another because they connect these roads, our rivers, our lakes, our gulfs and our oceans within our own land and to peoples in faraway countries.[1]

Name_____Date_____

My team members:

My bridge design:

I predict_____books will hold my bridge
Explain why your group chose this bridge design:[2,3]

Figure 18. Bridge design proposal

Name_____Date_____

Group Number	Sizes of books selected for bridge design	Prediction of number of books/weight held by design in cm	Actual number of books/weight held by design in cm
Group 1	_____	_____/___	_____/___
Group 2	_____	_____/___	_____/___
Group 3	_____	_____/___	_____/___
Group 4	_____	_____/___	_____/___
Group 5	_____	_____/___	_____/___
Group 6	_____	_____/___	_____/___
Group 7	_____	_____/___	_____/___

Figure 19. Bridge data handout[4]

NOTES

[1] Schlumberger Excellence in Education Development. (2015). Adapted from *Laboratory – Engineering Challenge: Clay boats*. Retrieved from http://www.planetseed.com/laboratory/clay-boats

[2] Adapted from Lesson on Bridge Building Assignment: Third Grade PAC. (2015). Retrieved from crebridgebuilding.pbworks.com/f/Bridge Building Assignment.doc

[3] Zweig-Rodriguez, R., & Capote, I. (n.d.). *When in Rome*. Miami, FL: Miami-Dade County Public Schools, Division of Mathematics and Science.

[4] Zweig-Rodriguez, R., & Capote, I. (n.d.). *When in Rome*. Miami, FL: Miami-Dade County Public Schools, Division of Mathematics and Science.

LESSON PLAN FAVORITES

M&M'S PRIMARY OR INTERMEDIATE LESSON PLAN

Background Information

Objects have observable properties, including size, weight, and temperature, which can be measured with rulers, balances, and thermometers. Objects are also described by the properties of the materials from which they are made and can be separated or sorted according to those properties. All materials exist in different states – solid, liquid, and gas – and can be changed from one state to another by heating and cooling. Substances that can be dissolved are solubles, and substances that dissolve a solute, a chemically different liquid, solid or gas, is a solvent, resulting in a solution.

Materials

Candy M&M's of all colors; five pieces of construction paper with a different colored M&M on each and then folded in half to represent a group nametag; five pieces of colored construction paper representing the five colors of M&M's (blue, green, red, yellow and orange), with *One M&M in Water* handout pasted to it; the *M&M Colors in Different Temperatures* handout; four bathroom size cups; Styrofoam plates; permanent marker; room temperature water; cold water; hot water; stopwatch; magnifying lens; and paper towels.

Engage

Teacher asks students: What are the three states of matter? And then asks them to describe each. Students then watch a brief video on the three states of matter, BrainPop, https://www.brainpop.com/science/matterandchemistry/statesofmatter/. After viewing the video, students are asked to describe what physical change is. After that, the teacher asks how many students love to eat M&M's, describing their favorite color. Once students call out their color choice, the teacher explains that they are going to observe M&M's in water.

Explore

Teacher divides class into collaborative learning groups of five to six students each, assigning roles such as project manager, assistant manager, materials manager, reporter/recorder, (combining the reporter/recorder into one role, depending on your class size), and team manager. Students may also select their jobs with the consensus of their peers in the group. The group discusses the responsibilities of each job. Each group decides which color M&M they want to investigate: blue, green, red, yellow, and orange. They are each given a nametag (see below) representing their colored M&M and also the colored construction paper (coinciding with their nametag and colored M&M) pasted with the *One M&M in Water* handout. Together, students read how they conduct the experiment. They complete it and observe their results for one minute while using their magnifying lens. Once students finish the first investigation, they will be given the same colored M&M and receive a new same-colored piece of construction paper with the investigation handout, *M&M Colors in Different Temperatures,* pasted to it. Students perform the experiment and observe what happens to the M&M's.

Explain

Groups share their results with the class, explaining physical change. In the first investigation, when an M&M is placed in water, the colored coating dissolves into the water in a relatively circular pattern around the M&M. The color comes off because it is soluble, which means that the water molecules and the molecules that make up the coloring have an attraction for each other and mix together. In the second investigation, the M&M color dissolves in hot water faster than it does in room temperature or cold water. The water molecules in hot water move faster and make more contacts with the color on the M&M's, resulting in more dissolving.

Elaborate

Students can use several different colors of M&M's or different liquids for both investigations and observe results. In the investigation with different temperatures of water, students could use common table salt instead of an M&M and observe results (salt does not dissolve much faster in hot water than in room temperature water).

Evaluate

Students make drawings based on the investigation and write in their science journals about their observations and the results, comparing one M&M in water to several M&M's in different temperatures of water. Students could also brainstorm together and write or draw other experiments they could conduct with M&M's.

Home Learning

Teacher passes out Skittles to all students and tells them to complete the experiment with water only. (The students can compare the results from M&M's and Skittles.) Students must report their results to the class.

Adaptations (For Exceptional Student Education)

Students only complete *One M&M in Water* investigation. (See below.) Students draw their observations.

Possible Connections to Other Disciplines

Integrates STEM, language arts, art.

Real World Connections

Students should be aware that the properties of a solvent helps remove stains from clothes such as in dry cleaning or washing clothes in the washing machine. Also, carbonated soft drinks get their "fizz" from dissolved carbon dioxide gas along with sugar and other flavorings in a water solution. It is better to keep carbonated drinks in a warm environment rather than in a refrigerator because when the cold can is opened the carbon dioxide quickly leaves but some still stays in the soft drink, which is what causes the explosion and spray we commonly see.[1]

One M&M in Water

- Fill a small bathroom-size cup with room temperature water. Pour the water into a Styrofoam plate so that it just covers the bottom. Add more water if necessary.
- Place one M&M in the center of the plate. Be careful to keep the water and candy as still as possible. Observe for about one minute. What do you observe?
- Empty the plate of water and candy into a bowl or sink. Dry the plate with a paper towel.

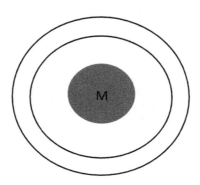

Figure 20. Model M&M plate

95

M&M Colors in Different Temperatures

- Use a permanent marker to trace around the top of a bathroom cup to draw a circle in the center of each plate. Turn the cup over and use the bottom to draw a smaller circle inside the larger one. Make a dot in the center of the smaller circle.
- Fill a small bathroom size sup with room temperature water and pour the water into a Styrofoam plate. Similarly, add hot water and cold water to each of two Styrofoam plates.
- At the same time, place the same colored M&M in the center of each plate. Wait one minute. What do you observe?

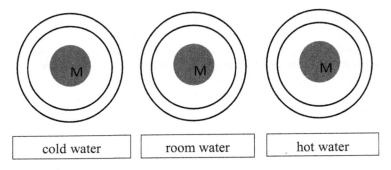

| cold water | room water | hot water |

Figure 21. Model M&M temperature plate

MYSTERY POWDER PRIMARY OR INTERMEDIATE LESSON PLAN

Background Information

Matter is everywhere. It has mass and takes up space. There are three forms of matter – solid, liquids, and gases – and they can be changed from one state to another, physical and chemical. In the physical state, the properties of matter change when they are related to the environment, such as temperature, pressure, and other physical forces. The matter may look or act differently but it is the same; the molecules do not change. In the chemical state, the bond between the atoms in a molecule are created or destroyed. The matter becomes completely different and does not come back. Hence, a new form of matter is created.

Materials

- Five white powders.
- Baking soda, cornstarch, sugar, and baking powder, each sealed in individual small plastic bags and labeled with stickers or magic markers as red, green, blue, yellow, and orange.
- Eye droppers.
- A small bottle of iodide (commonly known as iodine) for each group.
- Five Popsicle sticks, colored black with a permanent marker, one-half inch at each end. Each Popsicle stick also has a red, green, blue, yellow and orange sticker at the other end.
- The handouts for each group: *The Mystery Powder Directions, Class Properties Chart Predictions, Class Properties Chart, Laminated Circle Chart.*
- Paper towels.

Engage

Students engage in a discussion as teacher writes responses to the question, *What is Matter?* on the whiteboard. Students are lead to discuss what happens to matter when there is a physical change and teacher tells them they are going to solve the problem of the mystery powders.

Explore

Teacher divides class into collaborative learning groups of five or six students each, assigning roles such as project manager, assistant manager, materials manager, reporter, recorder, and team manager (combining the reporter/recorder into one role, depending on your class size). Students may also select their jobs with the consensus of their peers in the group. The group discusses the responsibilities of each job. All handouts are distributed and read together as a group. Each group completes the

Class Properties Prediction Chart and then begins the investigation. Placing a small amount of each powder on the colored marking at the end of Popsicle stick, which is designed to measure the amount of powder, one person in each group places that amount on the laminated circle and adds three drops of the liquid to test the powder and guess what it is. The same task sequence is repeated for each powder, each time completing the *Class Properties Chart*. As they explore the mystery powders, adding water and then iodide (iodine), teacher observes and answers questions as each group conducts their investigation.

Explain

Each group explains its predictions and results to the whole class and tells why and how the powder reacted to each liquid. Based on their evidence, students tell the names of each mystery powder.

Elaborate

Students can also use other liquids, such as milk and/or soda, to investigate what happens to each powder. They can change the powders to flour and/or powdered milk. Compare and contrast results of both.

Evaluate

The handout of the *Class Properties Chart* is collected and assessed.

Home Learning

Students draw and record findings of the experiment in their science journals.

Adaptations (For Exceptional Student Education)

Students conduct an investigation using water only and increase the amount of powder.

Possible Connections to Other Disciplines

Integrates science, mathematics, language arts.

Real World Connections

Students should be aware that when mixed with other ingredients, certain everyday powders like baking soda and baking powder affect how a cake will rise or if a cookie is flat or not. They should also be aware that when cornstarch and a liquid are mixed over heat, the combination thickens, which happens when we make certain foods, such as gravy.

The Mystery Powder Directions for the Investigation

First

Predict what will happen when you mix each powder with water. Write down your predictions.

Second

Use the red measuring stick and place one measure of the red mystery powder in the red test circle. Put three drops of water on the red mystery powder.

Third

Observe what happens and record on the Class Properties Chart.

Fourth

Repeat the second and third steps for each powder; the red, green, blue, yellow, and orange.

Fifth

Repeat all five steps using three drops of iodide (iodine) instead of water.

Sixth

Guess what the mystery powders are![2]

Class properties chart predictions

Mystery Powder	How it looks	How it smells	How it feels	Other Observations
Red				
Green				
Blue				
Yellow				
Orange				

Class properties chart

Mystery Powder	How it looks	How it smells	How it feels	Other Observations
Red				
Green				
Blue				
Yellow				
Orange				

Figure 22. Class properties charts

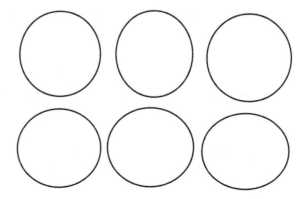

Figure 23. Laminated circle chart

PARACHUTES INTERMEDIATE LESSON PLAN

Background Information

Air is all around us and presses on everything; we call it air pressure. Bernoulli, a Swiss scientist, discovered what became known as Bernoulli's Principle, which states that air doesn't press as hard when it is moving. The faster the air moves, the less it presses. Airplanes provide an excellent example. Because an airplane wing is curved along the top and is flat on the bottom, the air has to move faster over the top, decreasing the air pressure on the top of the wing. This causes *lift* and helps the wing and the plane to stay up flying. Birds also are an excellent example of Bernoulli's Principle. Both parachutes and airplanes demonstrate air resistance, *drag*, which slows down the parachute or the airplane. *Drag* is the aerodynamic force that opposes an aircraft's motion through the air and is generated by every part of the airplane.

Materials

Paper napkins, paper towels, string, paper clip, pennies, stopwatch, measuring tape, graph paper, and the *How to Make a Parachute* handout.

Engage

Teacher asks students if they have ever flown on an airplane. If so, they describe their experiences. Students then view a video about flight on BrainPop: https://www.brainpop.com/technology/transportation/flight/preview.weml

Explore

Students are divided into partner-pairs. Students brainstorm how they think their parachute will fall: fast or slow, and why. Teacher distributes handouts and students create their own parachute; using three trials, they test its ability to fly and, recording the amount of time it takes to fall to the ground. Each time, they have to add a "passenger" to the paper clip and observe the results.

Explain

Students share their graph results and explain the number of passengers their parachute was able to "fly" and why the number of passengers affected the amount of time it needed to fall to the ground.

Elaborate

Students create another parachute using another type of napkin (lighter in weight and smaller in size) and test it for three trials, comparing it to their first parachute. Or,

101

students may use fishing line instead of string and test it for three trials, comparing it to their first parachute.

Evaluate

Teacher observes students working together and each partner-pair draws a bar graph on the whiteboard, recording their results of their first parachute. Teacher leads the class in a discussion about the reasons similarities and differences exist among the groups, and then collects bar graphs each partner-pair created.

Home Learning

Students create different kinds of paper airplanes and demonstrate how they fly, recording what they have learned about Bernoulli's Principle and air resistance in their science journals.

Adaptations (For Exceptional Student Education)

Students are given parachutes that have already been created and test them for three trials, recording their results.

Possible Connections to Other Disciplines

Integrates STEM, language arts, social studies.

Real World Connections

Students should be aware of airplanes, sky diving, hand gliding, and of a shower curtain that puffs inside the bathtub.

How to Make a Parachute

- Decide if you want a parachute from a paper napkin or a paper towel.
- Cut your string into four pieces, each one about 25 cm.
- Attach each piece of string to the corner of the napkin.
- Gather the four pieces of string together and attach to the paper clip.
- Add one penny and release your parachute.
- Explore the number of "passengers" (pennies) needed and how air affects the way a parachute flies.
- Have a parachute contest. Decide with your partner the manner and place of release of your parachute.
- Use a stopwatch to measure the amount of time it takes for each parachute to fall.

- Record and graph the results.
- Share with the entire class.[3,4]

ROCKET RACERS INTERMEDIATE LESSON PLAN

Background Knowledge

Newton's Third Law of Motion states that for every action there is an equal and opposite reaction. While it is possible to demonstrate this law with a balloon, constructing a rocket racer allows students to actually observe the action/reaction force in a practical way. The payload of the balloon rocket is the racer and the wheels reduce friction with the floor, which helps the racers move. Because each rocket racer is created differently in some way, they will travel at different distances and in unplanned directions. Students can then make modifications to improve their racer's efficiency.

Materials

Four pins, Styrofoam empty meat trays obtained at any local grocery store, masking tape, flexible straw, scissors, drawing compass, marker pen, small round balloon, ruler, ten-meter tape measure, and student handout.

Engage

Teacher draws a Venn Diagram on the whiteboard and asks students to identify similarities and differences between rockets and airplanes. Responses are written in each area of the two circles, including the middle section, which tells how both are the same. Discussion follows. Teacher explains that students are going to create a rocket racer and race them.

Explore

Teacher divides class into collaborative learning groups of five to six students each, assigning roles such as project manager, assistant manager, materials manager, reporter/recorder, (combining the reporter/recorder into one role, depending on your class size), and team manager. Students may also select their jobs with the consensus of their peers in the group. Students discuss the responsibilities of each job. Each group receives the materials and creates a rocket racer. Before cutting, teacher allows enough time for students to brainstorm about the arrangement of the different parts of the rocket racer on the tray. The teacher lays a track on the floor about ten meters long and students test their racers, measuring in ten centimeter intervals. Students create a data sheet, recording how far in centimeters their rocket racer moved over the three trials. They also draw their racer.

Explain

Each group demonstrates how their rocket racer races and why it moves as it does, giving reasons for its success or failure. Students must also relate it to Newton's Third Law of Motion and share their data and their drawing with the entire class.

Elaborate

Students race against each other in a rocket racer race. Students can use a different size balloon and test their racer to compare and contrast differences/similarities in its efficiency to move. Students can make a balloon-powered pinwheel by taping another balloon to a flexible straw and pushing a pin through the star and into a pencil eraser.

Evaluate

Teacher observes groups at work and collects data sheets as an assessment. Each group also creates a rocket racer test report that describes test runs and modifications (variables) that improved their racer's efficiency.

Home Learning

Students create a foldable about what they learned about rocket racers.

Adaptations (For Exceptional Student Education)

Teacher creates a model rocket racer before lesson begins and gives it to each partner pair to race.

Possible Connections to Other Disciplines

Integrates STEM, language arts, and, art.

Real World Connections

Students should be aware of exactly why seatbelts, headrests, and airbags in automobiles are really important and what happens when we sit in a chair – we are still subject to the constant acceleration of the Earth's gravity. It's trying to pull us down at 32 feet per second squared, but whatever we are sitting on, or standing on, stops us so we stick to that surface. If we take away that surface, gravitational acceleration takes over, until we encounter another surface, at which point, deceleration takes place.[5]

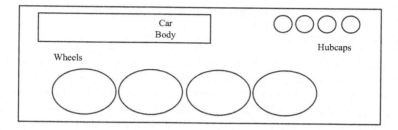

Figure 24. Rocket race model

- Lay out your pattern on a Styrofoam tray. Use a compass to draw the wheels. Cut out the wheels, hubcaps, and rectangle.
- Blow up the balloon and let the air out. Tape the balloon to the short end of a flexible straw and then tape the straw to the rectangle.
- Push pins through the hubcaps into the wheels and then into the edges of the rectangle.
- Blow up the balloon through the straw. Squeeze the end of the straw and place the racer on floor and let it go.[6]

SWINGERS INTERMEDIATE LESSON PLAN

Background Information

A pendulum is defined as any weight suspended on a string, rope, or other arm that is free to pivot from an anchor point. Think about a swing in the park. When the weight (the person sitting on the swing) is displaced from its natural resting position and released, the weight swings back and forth, completing each cycle in the same length of time as the previous cycle. If the weight of the pendulum, the length of the string, or the release position is changed, the number of swings also changes. These are called variables, defined as attributes that might affect the outcome of an experiment. There are *independent variables*, those attributes that the investigator changes on purpose, *dependent variables*, attributes that change by themselves because the student changes something in the investigation, and *controlled variables*, which are those that remain the same throughout the investigation.

As an example, if we investigated how much fertilizer a plant needs to grow, using at least three potted plants, the *independent* variable would be the amount of fertilizer given to each plant; the *dependent* variable would be the growth of each plant measured by its height and/or the growth of each plant measured by the number of leaves; and the *controlled* or constant variable would be the same amount of fertilizer placed into each plant, the same size pot used to grow each plant, and the same kind of plant in each pot.

Materials

Pennies, paper clips, string, meter tape, pencils, scissors, centimeter graph paper, paper, *Swingers*, *Swingers Number Line*, *How to Build a Swinger* handouts, LCD projector or Overhead Projector, access to Internet, numbered cards.

Engage

On the computer, students access the website: http://pbskids.org/zoom/games/pendulum/ and explore the characteristics of a pendulum. After 5–10 minutes, teacher gathers students to discuss what they observed. Teacher tells them that they are going to make their own pendulum, swinger, and observe how it works.

Explore

Teacher divides students into partner-pairs. Each group is given 50 cm string, two paper clips, two pennies, masking tape, scissors, and a meter measuring tape. Teacher asks students to create a swinger and share it with the class, at which point the teacher asks students how they decided what a swinger looks like, what they think they could do with a swinger, and how many swings they think it can swing in

15 seconds. Teacher distributes the handout, *How to Build a Swinger*, and explains that for purposes of this investigation, the swinger will be the same for each group.

Students then construct another swinger and test it by taping a pencil that sticks over the edge of their desk a few centimeters and then hangs the swinger by its loop from the pencil. Each group tests their swinger three times and counts the number of swings it makes in 15 seconds, recording their results. After five minutes, the teacher then asks the students to share their results by writing them on the whiteboard.

Next, the students create a different swinger; each group has a different length of string (passed out randomly or by students selecting a numbered card, previously prepared by the teacher). After testing their new swinger three times and recording results on graph paper, each group hangs their swinger on the *Swinger Number Line* and compares and contrasts the number of swings from the first swinger to the last one. Students should note and remark that the number of swings changed, creating a pattern: The teacher asks, "What do you observe on the number line?" "Do you see anything different?" "Similar?" The observations should be: the longer the string, the fewer the swings in 15 seconds; the shorter the string, the more swings in 15 seconds.

Explain

Students share their results with the whole class. Students realize that their results are different from other groups and have to explain why. Soon they realize that one cycle is different for each group and they discuss the variables. Teacher then suggests that each group use a standardized release position (meaning it begins at the same height and angle) and that one cycle is defined by the swinger swinging away and coming back. Students retest their swingers three times and share their new results.

Elaborate

Students change the variables of the swinger, such as the release position, to determine if the number of swings is different; or, they change the number of pennies inserted into the paper clip. Students create their own pendulum design and predict the number of swings in 15 seconds and/or the teacher challenges them to make a pendulum giving them a ball of string and having to decide the length of it with the notion that it will fit into the number line at a place where none is hanging.

Evaluate

Teacher observes students working together in partner pairs while helping them create their swingers and conduct the investigation. Students journal about their investigation in their science notebooks.

Home Learning

Students have to create a game about swingers that one of their peers can play in class. Teacher provides paper.

Adaptations (For Exceptional Student Education)

Students are given ready-made swingers.

Possible Connections to Other Disciplines

Integrates STEM, language arts, and social studies.

Real World Connections

Students should be aware of how we swing in a swing in the park, how a musician uses a metronome to play music, how clocks work, and how amusement park rides use pendulums.

Swingers

- Create your Swinger.
- Explore with your Swinger.
- Test your Swinger at least three times.
- Record your Results on Whiteboard Chart.
- Change your Swinger.
- Test your Swinger at least three times.
- Record your results on overhead/white board/graph paper.

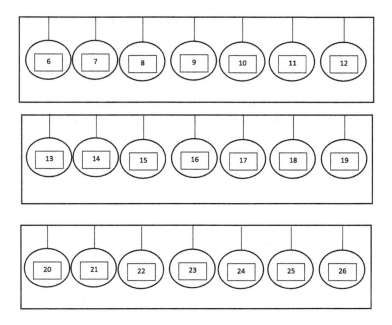

Figure 25. Swinger number line. Cut the three strips above and glue or tape them to a long strip of cardboard or heavy construction paper. Punch a hole under each number. Hang a paper clip in each hole to act as a hook

Materials	*Tools*
One string, 50 cm long One paper clip One penny Masking tape	One Meter tape One Pair of scissors

1. Tie the paper clip securely to one end of the string.
2. Measure 38 cm from the tip of the paper clip along the string. Fold the string back at exactly 38 cm.
3. Use a tiny piece of masking tape to make a loop. The loop should be large enough to hang a pencil. Re-measure to make sure the swinger is 38 cm from the tip of the paper clip to the top of the loop.
4. Clip a penny in the paper clip.[7-9]

Figure 26. How to build a swinger

OBSERVATIONS PRIMARY LESSON PLAN

Background Knowledge

Observing is an important part of everyday life. It is easily defined as gathering information about our surroundings, the world we live in, by using our five senses: smell, hear, touch, see, and taste. We draw inferences, which are explanations for an observation, based on our past experiences and prior knowledge. Our inferences often change when we make a new observation.

Materials

Hoola Hoops, 10 items found in the classroom, such as pencils, books, markers, construction paper, erasers, paper clips, plastic utensils, napkins, mathematical blocks/cubes, balloons, and so forth (five items of the same color and five of the same shape), magnifying lens, pennies, eyedroppers, the *Making Observation* handout, and paper towels.

Engage

Students are given mystery bags with 10 items in each bag. Teacher instructs them to make a Venn Diagram with the Hoola Hoops on the floor, and sort items accordingly. When students complete the task, teacher asks a variety of questions:

• What did you do?
• Why did you sort all the same colored items together?
• Why did you sort all the same shaped ones together?

Teacher leads students to discuss the meaning of observation and how important it is in our everyday life.

Explore

Teacher gives each student the *Making Observation* handout and tells students to draw from memory the front of a penny in Circle One. After some time, teacher passes a penny to each student and tells them to draw what they observe in the penny in Circle Two. Allowing more time, teacher passes magnifying lens to each student and tells them to use it to help draw their penny in Circle Three. Once students have completed that task, teacher passes out eyedropper and small cups of water and students place their penny on Circle Four with one drop of water and draw what they observe. Teacher allows ample time in between circle drawings for students to explore.

Explain

Teacher asks:

- What did you remember about the penny from your memory?
- How did that differ after you looked at the penny?
- After you used the magnifying lens?
- After you placed a drop of water on your penny?
- Why?

Teacher leads students to describe inferences they made based on their prior experiences and observations (depending on the age, teacher may not want to use the word "infer" but may simply imply it).

Elaborate

Students may substitute a drop of soda, such as cola, instead of water on their penny and compare results of their observations. Students may also substitute a dime or a quarter for the penny.

Evaluate

Teacher walks around the room, observing students' interest and ability to stay on task during the investigation. Students draw what they learned in their science journals.

Home Learning

Students write two to three sentences about three new observations they made on their penny.

Adaptations (For Exceptional Student Education)

Students may classify pennies by year and/or research why there are twelve columns on the building, what is on the steps, what the Latin phrase means, the name of the building on the back of the penny, and who is sitting on the chair.

Possible Connections to Other Disciplines

Integrates science, mathematics, language arts, social studies, and art.

Real World Connections

Students should be aware that we observe and classify objects all the time, whether it is the color of the clothes we wear, the buttons on a sweater, the food we eat, the kinds of cars we drive, the plants we see, or the animals we love.

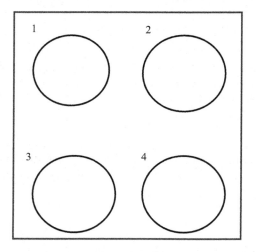

Figure 27. Making observation handout

FINGERPRINTING PRIMARY OR INTERMEDIATE LESSON PLAN

Background Information

Fingerprinting is the study of the friction pattern on our fingertips and is used for personal identification. The print is an impression left upon any surface where a finger has had contact under pressure. There are also toe-prints, footprints and lip-prints. Eight different types of fingerprint patterns exist, but for elementary students, the arch, loop and whorl are most commonly observed.

Figure 28. Fingerprints

Materials

Sticky Notes, pencils, science journals, white paper, transparent tape, three-columned poster board with pictures of Loop, Whorl, and Arch on bottom, one on the bottom of each column, hand lens/magnifying glasses, measuring tapes.

Engage

Teacher asks students to look at their fingers, specifically their forefinger, and describe what they observe. Once someone mentions fingerprints or lines, the teacher asks students what they are called. Teacher asks, "Why do we have fingerprints?" "What are they used for?" "Is there only one kind of fingerprint?" "How do you know?" Teacher then introduces poster board, displayed at the front of the room, with the three different types of fingerprints, asking students to see the differences and similarities. Then, students draw what they observed from their forefinger in their science journals or on a piece of paper.

Explore

Students are divided into partner-pairs and asked to rub their soft lead pencil to make a dark impression on a small piece of white paper, creating a black irregular box. Students then take a small piece of transparent tape and place it over the darkened fingertip. One sticky note is distributed to each student who then places the

113

small piece of transparent tape with the fingerprint onto the sticky note, lifting the transparent tape. The fingerprint should be seen on the sticky note. Using the hand lens and measuring tape, partners compare and contrast and identify their fingerprint.

Explain

Students place their sticky note fingerprint on the poster board in the correct column determined through observation and discussion, explaining why it was chosen as Loop, Whorl, or Arch.

Elaborate

Teacher asks students, "Which fingerprint is more common in our classroom?" "Why?" "Which fingerprint is less common in our classroom?" "Why?" "What do you think most people have?" "How do you know that?" Students can then do the same process on another finger or all of their fingers and identify them.

Evaluate

Students return and check their science journals or drawings and compare what they initially thought were Loop, Whorl, or Arch fingerprints to what their fingerprint actually looks like.

Home Learning

Students get the fingerprint of one person in their household and identify it, bringing it to class the next day. Depending on age level, students can research the history of fingerprinting on the computer.

Adaptations (For Exceptional Student Education)

Students create a fingerprint of their thumbs on an index card, labeling each card with the first letter of their name. Cards are mixed up and students have to guess which index card/fingerprint matches the person.

Possible Connections to Other Disciplines

Integrates science, technology, mathematics, language arts, social studies, art.

Real World Connections

Fingerprints are patterns found on the fingers, palms, toes, and lips of humans. They are also found on monkeys, apes, gorillas, orangutans and some kinds of birds. The ridges of fingerprints are lined with moisture, not oil, which causes a print to be made. Twins, triplets, and quadruplets all have completely different fingerprints. Prints can be dusted and lifted for up to several months after the impression is made and up to ten years if a laser is used. A fingerprint cannot be forged. Loops are the most common fingerprints, whorls are second most common, and arches are the least common fingerprints. DNA is another form of fingerprinting: The chemical structure of DNA in everyone is the same. The only difference is the order of the base pairs. As with fingerprinting, there are so many millions of base pairs in everyone's DNA that every person has a unique sequence. However, unlike fingerprinting, DNA fingerprinting cannot be altered.[10]

NOTES

[1] Kessler, J. H., & Galvan, P. M. (2003). Adapted from *Inquiry in action: Investigating matter through inquiry* (pp. 21–31). Washington, DC: American Chemical Society. Reprinted with permission from Inquiry in Action. Copyright 2003, American Chemical Society.

[2] Adapted from Science Matters. (2015). Retrieved from http://sbsciencematters.com/5th/physical/5.15MysteryPowders.pdf

[3] Science Kids: Fun Science and Technology for Kids. (2015). *Design and test a parachute.* Retrieved from http://www.sciencekids.co.nz/experiments/freefall.html

[4] Kids Activities Blog. (2012). *Make a parachute: Kids parachute {creates} resistance experiments.* Retrieved from http://kidsactivitiesblog.com/18461/make-a-parachute-kids-parachute-resistance-experiments

[5] Thompson, B. (2015, September 20). *Answer* (p. 1). Retrieved from http://quest.nasa.gov/saturn/qa/new/Effects_of_speed_and_acceleration_on_the_body.txt

[6] Adapted from NASA. (n.d.). *Rockets: A teacher's guide with activities in science, mathematics and technology.* Washington, DC: NASA.

[7] Lesson adapted from Pendulum Experiment. (2015). Retrieved from https://explorable.com/pendulum-experiment

[8] Highlights Kids. (2015). *Science experiments: Make a pendulum.* Retrieved from https://explorable.com/pendulum-experiment

[9] FOSS Variables, Second Edition (2005). Developed at the Lawrence Hall of Science and published and distributed by Delta Education. Copyright © The Regents of the University of California. Used with permission.

[10] Lesson adapted from https://www.teachervision.com/tv/printables/TCR/1576903443_80-81.pdf and http://www.discoveryeducation.com/teachers/free-lesson-plans/the-science-of-forensics.cfm

CONCLUSION

> The important thing is not to stop questioning. Curiosity has its own reason for existing. One cannot help but be in awe when he contemplates the mysteries of eternity, of life, of the marvelous structure of inquiry.
>
> Albert Einstein

Science is everywhere – we see it, hear it, feel it and smell it every day of our lives. While some delight in teaching science, others do not; likewise, while some love learning science, others do not. What's your position? Are you a teacher who sets your curriculum based on science concepts? Do you include STEM topics? Do you integrate language arts, social studies, and mathematics into science? Or do you teach language arts, social studies, and mathematics as isolated from scientific concepts? Do you follow the Next Generation Science Standards or the Common Core Standards with *science* in mind?

Specifically, do you provide ample opportunities for your students to explore, discover, conduct hands-on investigations, think critically, and problem solve? Do you provide them with scenarios where they can connect scientific concepts to their daily life? Do you include technology when you are planning your lessons? Now is the time to explore those questions and then overcome any fears you may have about learning and teaching science.

Why is science teaching so important right here and right now? The answer isn't difficult or complex. Research results indicate our students, in general, are not performing or reaching their potential in science knowledge. We owe it to our students, and to the future of our world, to inspire our children to develop their own natural curiosity. That's what science teaching is all about.

From the start, my purpose in this book was to present ten easy steps to assist you in creating an effective science curriculum. These steps include techniques to give you the skills to build, adapt, and construct a worthwhile and meaningful science program. The steps and techniques certainly are not all inclusive, but they provide a place to begin. By now, I hope you see that you don't have to be a scientist or science "diva" to implement these educational strategies. I intentionally made them simple and easy to follow so that you can target *all* elementary school learners, whether they live in large urban communities, small towns, or rural areas.

This book arose from my lifelong belief that science should be fun! So, try to create a community of learners gathered together in a positive atmosphere filled with passion and enthusiasm for science. This environment is one that promotes inquiry, communication, and a love for learning all things relevant to science and the notion of science. I hope you will inspire your students to enjoy the science phenomena they observe everyday and furnish them with opportunities to use critical thinking skills to solve problems that can apply in the future – their personal and shared future.

It's also my hope that you work to make your students aware of rapidly changing technology, whether it involves researching a question or just learning about a specific science concept. In this way, you'll promote their curiosity and welcome their questions and quest to find answers, which then lead to more questions. Your teaching will undoubtedly help them to understand the necessity to conserve our natural resources and create a better life for themselves and their communities as they grow older.

Finally, your teaching can instill a sense of mystery about science as your students learn how nature and technology work, the way the natural world changes and grows, and why the things others have invented are designed in a certain fashion. When you find the time and the energy to pursue a love of science learning over the long run, you are your students' role model, one they will remember as the *best* science teacher ever! That's my dream for you.

APPENDICES

ELEMENTS OF A SCIENCE FAIR PROJECT[1]

RESOURCES

- http://www.sciencebuddies.org/science-fair-projects/project_ideas.html
- http://www.education.com/science-fair/
- http://www.all-science-fair-projects.com/

PROJECT STATEMENT

This statement is always written in the form of a question and directs the student's investigation. A good problem statement will convey a mental image of how the question can be investigated.

HYPOTHESIS

After gathering information about the topic, students should make an educated guess about what they think the answer to the question may be. *Example: Paper towel X will absorb the most water.*

ACKNOWLEDGEMENTS

Students should make a list of any people who may have helped them, including their parents.

ABSTRACT

This is a short summary of the entire project, which must include purpose, procedure, and results. It should be limited to 100 words or less for primary grades and 250 words for intermediate grades. After the title, it is usually the first thing the judges look at.

REFERENCES

This is a list of all the books, magazines, and other sources the investigator uses. *Example: author's last name, first initial, title of the book, publisher, year published, where published, pages used.*

TITLE

The project title should provide information about the topic being studied, and may consist of the actual problem statement. However, the investigation will appear more interesting if the title creates curiosity and interest.

MATERIALS

Preferably presented in column form, list all the materials used. Express quantities and amounts of materials in metric units, unless another form is appropriate.

PROCEDURE

List the procedure step by step, in the same manner as the materials. Always include amounts involved and the *number of trials (at least three)*.

VARIABLES

These include all factors affecting the investigation. A *manipulated* variable is the item that is intentionally changed in order to test it. A *responding* variable is what is changed in response to the *manipulated* variable. *Constant* variables are all other factors in the investigation that must remain the same.

DATA

All information collected should be kept in a log and presented in an easy-to-understand manner. Graphs and charts should be used to show the reader what the student observed during the experiment.

PICTURES/PHOTOGRAPHS

Student may include photos of the experiment; however, the investigator should not be photographed.

RESULTS

The investigator should state the findings of the experiment based on data observed and carefully analyzed. *Example: According to the data...*

CONCLUSION

A statement made on whether the results supported the hypothesis . The investigator should discuss how specific data derived from the experiment supported the hypothesis and describe problems that might have affected the results.

APPLICATIONS

Students should explain why this experiment was important, that is, *relevant to real-life situations.*

REPORT

The report includes title page, abstract, table of contents, problem statement, background information, hypothesis, experiment, materials, procedure, variables, data, results, conclusion, applications, acknowledgements, and references.

Table 1. Science fair project display standard-sized science fair board

PROBLEM STATEMENT	PROJECT TITLE	RESULTS
THE QUESTION YOU ARE ASKING AND TRYING TO SOLVE	TITLE SHOULD BE SHORT AND ATTENTION-GETTING	A STATEMENT AS TO WHAT YOU FOUND ACCORDING TO YOUR DATA
	MATERIALS A LIST OF EVERYTHING YOU USED	
HYPOTHESIS THE ANSWER YOU THINK YOU WILL GET FOR THE ABOVE QUESTION	**PROCEDURE** A STEP-BY-STEP EXPLANATION OF WHAT YOU DID, USED, AND HOW YOU USED IT	**CONCLUSION** ANSWERS WHY YOU HAVE THE RESULTS FROM WHAT YOU DID. RELATE YOUR RESULTS TO YOUR HYPOTHESIS
ABSTRACT MAXIMUM ONE PAGE SUMMARY	**VARIABLES** ALL OF THE FACTORS THAT AFFECT YOUR INVESTIGATION (FOR EXAMPLE, AMOUNT OF LIGHT, TYPE OF SOIL, AMOUNT OF LIQUID USED, ETC.)	**APPLICATIONS** ANSWERS HOW YOUR EXPERIMENT MIGHT HELP ALL OF US
REFERENCES MINIMUM THREE (BOOKS, MAGAZINE, INTERNET, INTERVIEWS)	**DATA** THE PICTURES, DATA, TABLES, DIAGRAMS, AND OTHER SUPPORT MATERIAL YOU HAVE AS PROOF OF DOING THE PROJECT	**REPORT** A TITLE PAGE, ABSTRACT, TABLE OF CONTENTS AND ALL THE INFORMATION FROM THIS BOARD WITH REFERENCES

The following evaluation serves as a possible tool for assessing science fair projects:

Science Fair Project Evaluation for Initial Judging[2]

Primary and Intermediate Grades

Project Number:_____   Project Color:_____
Rate Project on a 1–5 Scale: 1 = LOW   5 = HIGH

Problem statement is specific and facilitates investigation.	1	2	3	4	5
Number of trials is adequate to support results/conclusions.	1	2	3	4	5
Data are sufficient, well organized and clearly presented.	1	2	3	4	5
Variables are listed and accurate.	1	2	3	4	5
Accurate interpretations of data are stated in results.	1	2	3	4	5
Report is present.	1	2	3	4	5
Display is well-organized and easy to follow.	1	2	3	4	5
Project follows scientific method.	1	2	3	4	5
The applications are appropriate and applied to everyday life.	1	2	3	4	5
Oral presentation is clear/well-prepared.	1	2	3	4	5
Presenter's knowledge and use of resources are complete.	1	2	3	4	5

*Total Points*_____

NOTES

[1] Elements adapted from Miami Dade County Public Schools, Division of Mathematics and Science (n.d). Retrieved from http://science.dadeschools.net/elementaryScienceFair/documents/2014-2015/2014-2015%20Elementary%20Science%20Fair%20Handbook-2.pdf

[2] If the science projects are going to be displayed school wide then each project should be labeled with a sticky colored numbered dot – the colored dot indicates the grade level and the number indicates to whom the project belongs. Assign project numbers on your classroom list on the day when the projects are due. If the projects are only displayed within the classroom, each project should have a sticky numbered dot so that the teacher is unbiased in judging it.

TEACHER-MADE ASSESSMENTS

Informal formative assessments demonstrate students' true understanding of a scientific concept. The examples below can be revised and adapted to meet the needs of your students, depending on their grade level and abilities. They are simply guidelines for you to use as you assess and evaluate how much your students are learning.

TEACHER OBSERVATION

Teacher casually walks around the classroom, taking notes about how students are learning, asking them questions as they work in cooperative learning groups. The teacher may use an observation rubric (see example below), write anecdotal notes, or complete a simple checklist (see example below).

Table 2. Classroom observation rubric

	Target	Acceptable	Unacceptable
Cognitive Learning (1.000, 10%)	All students appear to problem solve to understand the science content.	Most students appear to problem solve to understand the science content.	Some students appear to problem solve to understand the science content.
Science Process Skills/Practices (1.000, 10%)	Students are using all their science process skills/ practices, observe infer, predict, measure, communicate, predict and classify, to explore and investigate and reach a better understanding of the science content.	Students are using most of their science process skills/practices, observe infer, predict, measure, communicate, predict and classify, to explore and investigate and reach a better understanding of the science content.	Students are using a few of their science process skills/ practices, observe infer, predict, measure, communicate, predict and classify, to explore and investigate and reach a better understanding of the science content.

(Continued)

125

Table 2. (Continued)

	Target	Acceptable	Unacceptable
Cooperative Learning Groups (1.000, 10%)	Students are working well together, demonstrating teamwork and incorporating good decision-making while each are following their role responsibilities.	Students are somewhat working well together, demonstrating teamwork and incorporating good decision-making while some are following their role responsibilities.	Students are not working well together, demonstrating teamwork and incorporating good decision-making while none are following their role responsibilities.
Engage in Learning (1.000, 10%)	Students are totally involved, engaged, and enthusiastic about the science topic.	Students are involved, engaged, and somewhat enthusiastic about the science topic.	Students are not involved, engaged or enthusiastic about the science topic.
Science Discourse (1.000, 10%)	Students are talking to each other, sharing ideas and trying to reach a solution.	Students are somewhat talking to each other, sharing some ideas and attempting to reach a solution.	Students are not talking to each other and not sharing any ideas to reach a solution.
Integrate STEM (1.000, 10%)	Students are integrating STEM topics into the lesson.	Students are integrating two of the STEM topics into the lesson.	Students are not integrating any of the STEM topics into the lesson.
Critical Thinking (1.000, 10%)	Students are thinking critically, making sound judgments, to reach a joint decision.	Students are somewhat thinking critically, attempting to make sound judgments to reach a joint decision.	Students are not thinking critically and not attempting to make a joint decision.
NGSS Standards/ Common Core Standards (1.000, 10%)	Students are driven by the standards/cross cutting concepts and the nature of science.	Students are somewhat driven by the standards/ cross cutting concepts and the nature of science.	Students are not driven by the standards/cross cutting concepts and the nature of science.
Manipulatives (1.000, 10%)	All students are using the manipulatives to help them solve the problem.	Most students are using the manipulatives to help them solve the problem.	A few students are using the manipulatives to help them solve the problem.
Handouts (1.000, 10%)	Students are completing the assigned handouts based on the evidence.	Students are somewhat completing the assigned handouts based on the evidence.	Students are not completing the assigned handouts and have not gathered any evidence.

Table 3. The 5Es teacher observation rubric[1]

	Target	Acceptable	Unacceptable
Engage (1.000, 20%)	Many students discuss their ideas and experiences about the concept and are curious at the same time. They appear engaged in the science content and anticipate the next step in the process of learning more.	Some students discuss their ideas and experiences about the concept and are curious at the same time. Some appear engaged in the science content and anticipate the next step in the process of learning more.	Few students discuss their ideas and experiences about the concept and few are curious at the same time. Few appear engaged in the science content and do not anticipate the next step in the process of learning more.
Explore (1.000, 20%)	Many students eagerly explore the concept using the provided manipulatives. During this phase, they may identify and develop concepts, which further enhances their process of learning.	Some students eagerly explore the concept using the provided manipulatives. During this phase, some may identify and develop concepts, which further enhances their process of learning.	Few students eagerly explore the concept using the provided manipulatives. During this phase, few may identify and develop concepts, which further enhances their process of learning.
Explain (1.000, 20%)	Many students explain what they have learned about the concept and can demonstrate new skills or behaviors.	Some students explain what they have learned about the concept and can demonstrate new skills or behaviors.	Few students explain what they have learned about the concept and cannot demonstrate new skills or behaviors.
Elaborate (1.000, 20%)	Many students can practice what they have learned about the concept because they have developed a deeper and broader understanding of it. As a result, they gain more information about the concept and appear to learn about other areas related to it.	Some students can practice what they have learned about the concept because they have developed a somewhat deeper and broader understanding of it. As a result, some gain more information about the concept and appear to learn about other areas related to it.	Few students can practice what they have learned about the concept because they have not developed a deeper and broader understanding of it. As a result, few gain more information about the concept and do not appear to learn about other areas related to it.
Evaluate (1.000, 20%)	Many students assess and evaluate their understanding of the concept, which may be accomplished as an individual, in a cooperative learning group or by the teacher.	Some students assess and evaluate their understanding of the concept, which may be accomplished as an individual, in a cooperative learning group or by the teacher.	Few students assess and evaluate their understanding of the concept, which may be accomplished as an individual, in a cooperative learning group or by the teacher.

Table 4. Sample generic observation template

Attribute	Yes	No
Students address their misconceptions.		
Students engage in science discourse.		
Students engage in critical thinking.		
Students work cooperatively with each other to explore and discover.		
Students are using some form of technology to help them investigate.		
Students apply data as evidence to problem solve.		
Students complete handouts with graphs/charts/tables.		
Students present their results.		

Table 5. Checklist. Sample generic science content template

Solids, Liquids and Gases	Yes	No
Students understand the difference between liquids and solids.		
Students understand the difference between liquids and gases.		
Students understand the difference between solids and gases.		
Students discuss the definition of each among themselves.		
Students use the manipulatives to help them distinguish each state of matter.		
Students work cooperatively with each other in learning about solids, liquids, and gases.		
Students observe, predict, infer, and measure to gather evidence about their investigation on the three states of matter.		
Students are using some technology to help them understand the three states of matter.		
Students use their mathematics skills to help them understand the three states of matter.		
Students analyze data from their investigation and interpret it to reach a consensual agreement on their investigation of the three states of matter.		
Students complete the handouts on the three states of matter with graphs/charts/tables.		
Students present their results as a team.		
Students apply what they learned about solids, liquids and gases to everyday life.		

MODELS

Possible Performance Assessment Models

- An airplane or rocket out of 8.5 × 11 paper;
- A planet created in paper Mache/rubber ball/balloon;
- A model on how magnets attract;
- Dioramas of:
  - Different ecosystems, such as oceans, rainforests, deserts, tundra, fresh water;
  - The food chain;
  - The food web;
  - digestive system;
  - The seasons.
- Different kinds of clouds;
- The three states of matter;
- The water cycle;
- Different kinds of light, such as translucent, transparent, opaque;
- Different forms of electricity, such as static and current;
- Different animals based on classification: vertebrates, invertebrates, species;
- How sound is created;
- Properties of sound, such as pitch and volume and how it travels;
- Properties of rocks, such as sedimentary, metamorphic, igneous;
- The process of erosion and/or weathering.

STUDENT-MADE ASSESSMENTS

Journaling and Science Notebooks, See Step Four

Portfolios.   Teachers assign students to compile their own portfolios based on the work that has been created throughout the school year. Portfolios are a collection of class work products created over a period of time that showcase ongoing learning of scientific topics. It is the responsibility of each and every student to choose what items should be included in their portfolio and, consequently, they become active participants in their learning and evaluation. They choose their best work to place in their portfolios; it should show their progress in understanding and developing an interest in scientific concepts studied during the school year. Selections can be placed every nine weeks or at the end of the school year. They can be written reports, drawings, graphs, and charts, reflections on videos, information on science websites, and/or reflections on field trips, and handouts completed in class individually or within a cooperative learning group. The following is a simple portfolio assessment template:

Table 6. Portfolio assessment

	Target	Acceptable	Unacceptable
Appearance is neat and tidy.			
Well-organized and sequentially ordered.			
Growth is evident in science content.			
Language mechanics are precise and correct.			
Appears to understand science content.			
Drawings, writings, and graphs/charts, are appropriate for grade level.			
Demonstrates creativity and originality.			

NOTE

[1] Corporation for Public Broadcasting (2002). *Enhancing education: The 5 E's.* Retrieved from http://enhancinged.wgbh.org/research/eeeee.html

LEARNING RESPONSIBILITIES[1]

The following are the titles and responsibilities assigned to cooperative learning groups in your science classroom. Each member should understand the overall role and tasks of each position.

Project Director

- Meets with the teacher for special directions and receives individual team members' assignments.
- Instructs team members about their assignments.
- Insures that everyone participates.
- Informs teacher when experiment is completed.
- Assists with experiment.
- Records data from experiment.
- Helps with clean-up.

Assistant Director

- Distributes a copy of the experiment to each team member.
- Hands out and collects job badges.
- Keeps records of team members' jobs.
- Collects and organizes written reports.
- Assists with experiment as assigned by the Project Director.
- Records data from experiment.
- Helps with clean-up.

Materials Manager

- Gathers materials and equipment for the experiment.
- Returns materials and equipment to the proper place.
- Checks area at clean-up time.
- Assists with experiment as assigned by the Project Director.
- Records data from experiment.
- Assists with clean-up.

Reporter

- Reads orally the procedure of the experiment.
- Reports orally to the class the team's finding (after all teams have completed the experiment).
- Assists with experiment as assigned by the Project Director.
- Records data from experiment.
- Helps with clean-up.

Team Member

- Assists with experiment.
- Records data from experiment.
- Helps with clean-up.

NOTE

[1] Learning responsibilities; Student roles. (n.d.). Adapted from Miami Dade County Public Schools, Division of Mathematics and Science.

THE EVERGLADES MODEL

Lesson Plans and Interactive Activities in a Place-Based Setting

PARK (Parks as Resources for Knowledge) is a nationwide program used for a variety of programs within the U.S. National Park Service. "Fire in the Pine Rocklands PARK" is a curriculum designed for preservice teachers, referred to as teacher-students, but it's easily adapted for all grade levels. Based on an essential question that focuses on prescribed fires in a national park, it incorporates inquiry-based learning and the 5Es, and serves as a model for discovery, critical thinking, and problem-solving. Many of the hands-on, interactive handouts can be incorporated into science units, such as ecosystems and the environment, specifically topics such as plants, fire, the impact of the water cycle, and living and non-living things. Although the curriculum was devised for informal science learning, attending a field trip, the activities could be accomplished within the classroom. Many of those activities integrate STEM topics as well as language arts, social studies, and art.

A team of educators from a local college and Everglades National Park staff from the Education and Fire Management departments initiated the program in 2009; its goals are to introduce, prepare, and educate future teachers about the national parks and their ecosystems and the resources they provide. This knowledge would allow them to effectively pass on what they learned to their future students. The idea involved learning to investigate key scientific content and inquiry skills, a model for science inquiry, in an outdoor learning environment, hence place-based, along with exposing preservice teachers to extensive resources such as scientists' expertise, curriculum materials, and opportunities to attend and fund field trips.

A similar program had been established at the Golden Gate National Park and because of its success, a grant requiring a college professor, a park educator, and a scientist was written by the National Park Foundation in order to extend the program to other parks in the country. Supported by the Toyota Foundation, a three year project was approved to focus on developing a strong partnership between National Park educational staffs and higher education teacher – education faculty. This partnership and programs would provide preservice teachers with hands-on activities, inquiry-based learning, place-based educational experiences, and embedded assessments aligned to state standards.

In its early developmental stages, I was asked to brainstorm ideas on how to teach the curriculum through an inquiry-based approach. As an elementary school teacher and adjunct professor, I was eager to teach my preservice teachers (teacher-students) about the importance of the Everglades and its significance to survival in South Florida, especially its preservation for future generations. Throughout my teaching experiences, I came to realize that my preservice teachers were unaware of the importance of the Everglades in the South Florida region. Many had not even visited the park.

Together, the team developed inquiry-based lesson plans, strategies to teach the curriculum, student worksheets, maps, historical material, a journal and resource guide, a list of necessary materials to teach the program, such as tools for experiments, photos of foliage and fauna of the ecosystems, surveys, special nametags for teacher-students working in cooperative learning groups, posters, assessment tools, homework assignments, and PowerPoint presentations. Divided into three sections – pre-site, onsite, and post-site – the curriculum comparing the Pine Rocklands habitat to the Hammock habitat was embedded into a science methods course offered at the local college, and it continues to be taught.

The lesson plan is adaptable and can be changed to meet the needs of you and your students, at whatever grade level. In including this lesson plan, my intention is to help you create science-related topics and develop lessons relevant to your class size and class setting.

The funds to transport my teacher-students to and from the park were covered through the grant but there may be local resources you can access that will help with transportation to your nearby park or preserve. If you wish to use the materials as an indoor curriculum, you certainly can adjust and modify the lesson plans accordingly.

As you will see, the material below is relevant to both teachers learning to present this curriculum and to the students they will teach in the future. It is written as an instructor's guide to follow in order to teach the topics onsite. However, you can adapt the activities and incorporate them in an indoor or outdoor field trip. Be assured that you can teach this lesson to your elementary students. The activities are the same sequence that you can follow with your elementary students or, if you wish, you can teach them in the sequence that would most benefit you and your students. Some resources are available as free downloads you'll find by visiting the following website: www.nps.gov/ever/learn/education.

The onsite Lesson Plan is showcased below:

ONSITE LESSON PLAN: ECOLOGY OF FIRE IN THE PINE ROCKLANDS

Background Information

Observation and inference, the basic science process skills/practices, are the focus of the onsite visit and serve to segue into learning why some ecosystems within the Everglades National Park need fire to maintain themselves. Teacher-students will attend a field trip to Everglades National Park, Long Pine Key Nature Trail.

Teacher-students will:

- learn how to incorporate inquiry-based learning as a strategy for teaching;
- learn how to incorporate the 5-E Learning Cycle Model Approach as a science teaching strategy;
- understand the science process skills /practices of the Next Generation Science Standards and incorporate Common Core Standards.

Teacher-students will:

- learn to differentiate between observation and inference;
- understand the basic needs of an ecosystem;
- understand the relationship between fire ecology and habitat conservation in the Pine Rockland ecosystem;
- learn how habitats develop over time, specifically in the Everglades National Park;
- work with tools to observe and measure how plants grow;
- work together in cooperative learning groups to reach a viable conclusion about the Essential Question;
- learn how to respond to the Essential Question, How does fire impact an ecosystem?

Teacher-students will depart on a bus from the college campus. On the bus, teacher will distribute prepared habitat-pictured nametags defining group responsibilities (see below), such as Park Ranger, Field Tech, Safety Officer, Timekeeper, Interpreter, Recorder, as well as photo release forms.

Upon arrival, a Park Ranger will welcome teacher-students to Everglades National Park, introduce staff members, review safety procedures, present the Essential Question, review lesson plan for day, site selection, and lead brief discussion on observations and inferences and concepts learned during the pre-site session. Clipboards are distributed to each teacher-student and teacher-students form their cooperative learning group according to their habitat-pictured nametags and consensually decide who has each job/responsibility.

Park Ranger. The park ranger serves as the spokesperson for the group while also making sure the resource is protected by not littering, picking plants, or removing anything from the park.

Field Technician. The field tech is responsible for handling any instruments and teaching others in the group how to use them.

Safety Officer. Group safety is the safety officer's first priority including looking out for solution holes, making sure everyone is properly dressed, identifying potential hazards, and reminding everyone to keep hydrated.

Timekeeper.   The timekeeper monitors the time given for each activity and ensures everyone stays on task.

Recorder.   The recorder reads the directions to the group and maintains the official group record in the field journal.

Materials

- Clipboards and pencils;
- Examples of grasses/herbs and needles/broadleaves;
- Pine Rockland Field Journal;
- densitometer;
- light meter;
- ground cover frame;
- measuring tape/ruler;
- poster paper;
- markers;
- portable easels.

Engage (35 minutes)

Teacher-students will have 10 minutes to explore the area in pairs, recording their observations and inferences on clipboards provided by the Park Ranger. They will share their findings in a brief discussion. The Park Ranger then displays various examples of grasses/herb and needles/broadleaves and introduces the Pine Rockland Field Journal, which provides hand-outs, important illustrations, and detailed questions to be answered in the concluding activity. Teacher-students are already divided into cooperative learning groups of four-five persons per group, according to the habitat-pictured nametags (Grasses, Herbaceous, Shrubs, Pines, Broadleaf, Wildflowers) given at random on bus; relevant instructions are communicated by the Park Ranger regarding the layout of color-coded centers, separate locations or guided activities, that were pre-labeled – Fire Adaptations, Habitat, Shrub Height, Sunlight, and Vegetation (see below) – located throughout the two habitats and previously set up prior to arrival in the Pine Rockland and Hammock habitats.

Explore, Explain, and Elaborate (80 minutes; approximately 20 minutes per activity)

Teacher-students are directed to participate in each center on a rotating basis in both habitats. Park Rangers and professor will be assigned to one center to guide teacher-students in their investigation.

- Area A (center) *Fire Adaptations*

An adaptation is an adjustment or change in behavior, physiology, or structure of an organism to become more suited to its environment.

Table 7. Pine Rockland fire adaptations data handout[1]

Evidence of fire	Example 1	Example 2	Example 3
Description			
Is it living or dead?			
How can you tell?			
What killed it or enabled it to survive?			

- Area B (center) *Habitat*

Table 8. Pine Rockland habitat data handout[2]

Habitat characteristics	Deer	Bird	Lizard	Butterfly
Food What do you see that this animal might eat?				
Water Where can this animal find water?				
Shelter What can this animal use for shelter?				
Space What area can this animal use for space?				

- Area C (center) *Shrub Height*

Table 9. Pine Rockland and Hammock shrub height data handout[3]

Plant name	Area 1 – Pine Rockland	Switch areas	Area 2 – Hammock
	Height		Height
Plant 1			
Plant 2			
Plant 3			
Average			

- Area D (center) *Sunlight and Vegetation*

Table 10. Pine Rockland and Hammock sunlight and vegetation data handout[4]

	Area 1 Pine Rockland	Area 2 Hammock
Percentage of canopy cover		
Predominant tree type (broadleaf or needles)		
Light through canopy		
Percentage of grass & herbaceous ground cover		

Table 11. Evaluation data handout[5]

Which area has more...	Area 1 Pine Rockland	Area 2 Hammock
... canopy cover?		
... sunlight?		
... ground cover?		

Teacher-students will have approximately 15–20 minutes per center. Tools for each will be available for teacher-students to manipulate, gather evidence, record data, and elaborate on findings. When possible, measurement should be in centimeters. Results will be recorded in teacher-students' journals under the appropriate handout.

Evaluate (40 minutes)

Cooperative learning groups will work together at available onsite picnic tables to answer their assigned question listed in their Pine Rockland Field Journal. They will prepare a poster, based on one question assigned to them from the Pine Rockland Field Journal, for presentation, which indicates the evidence they gathered during their investigations. They will use other resource guides provided to them for additional information. Teacher-students will share with whole group.

Home Learning

Assignment will be reviewed and assigned to be completed prior to post-site visit.
Please conduct the following survey:

*Write a brief paragraph to summarize your answer to the Essential Question,
Survey three (3) people and ask them the following question: What is your*

opinion of fire in Everglades National Park. Discuss with them what you have learned about fire in the Pine Rocklands habitat. Did your discussion change their point of view? Write each response and record the results of your discussion.

Teacher-students will board buses, depart for college campuses, and complete comment cards with the following Everglades evaluation questions:

- What did you learn today?
- How do you think fire plays a role in maintaining the Pine Rockland's habitat?
- How do you think fire play a role in maintaining the Hammock's habitat?

Adaptation (For Exceptional Student Education)

- Provide more hands-on activities.
- Provide sufficient visuals to engage learner.
- Integrate more technology into lesson.
- Provide more access to textbooks and other references about the Everglades National Park.
- Encourage more peer-tutoring.

Possible Connections to Other Disciplines

Integrates mathematics, science, mathematics, engineering, technology (STEM), and language arts.

Real World Connections

Specifically, teacher-students should learn that the hammock habitat is a unique and significant ecosystem on its own and that it is not only the end result of a succession of a Pineland, but a Pineland without fire can succeed to a hammock. Teacher-students should also be aware that the Everglades is an important resource for living and surviving in South Florida because it is an extensive, complex, and renowned wetland ecosystem, important to the entire country. Additionally, it is home to a multitude of plants, animals, and birds – both resident and migratory – that live in some habitats not found anywhere else on the North American continent. As a result, it is crucial to preserve and conserve it for present and future generations.

ACKNOWLEDGEMENTS

Thank you to Miami Dade College and Everglades National Park, my co-partners in the development of this curriculum:

Everglades National Park, PARKS, Parks as Resources of Knowledge, Teachers Program at Golden Gate National Park, http://www.nps.gov/goga/learn/education/park-teachers-essay.htm

NOTES

[1] In Area A, look for 3 different examples that indicate evidence of fire in the Pine Rockland habitat and write the description in the table.

[2] In Area B, observe what animals might use for food, water, shelter, and space in the Pine Rockland habitat. You may use existing knowledge to infer answers that you are unable to observe.

[3] In Area C, there are three individual shrubs of the same species in Pine Rockland habitat and the Hammock habitat that are flagged to identify them (six plants total). Collect data to compare and contrast the same plant species growing in two different habitats:

- Record the plant name from the identification tag.
- Measure the plants from the ground to the tallest green leaf with the measuring tape.
- Record the height in centimeters in the table below. Be sure to include both the number and the unit of measurement (e.g. 160 cm).
- You may calculate the average later, after completing your fieldwork.
- Record any observations about the plants or the habitat in the space provided.
- Move to the 2nd area and repeat steps 2–5.

[4] In Area D, using the densitometer, estimate and record the percentage of canopy cover in the table. Record the dominant tree type in the canopy. Use the light meter to measure and record the amount of light penetrating the canopy. Include the units (fc = foot candles). Use the ground cover frame (0.5 m^2) to estimate and record the percentage of grass and herbaceous plants covering the ground. Record any additional observations below.

[5] Evaluate your results: place an "X" in the correct column to answer the questions.

VALUABLE WEBSITES/RESOURCES

ANIMATED VIDEOS

- BrainPOP. www.brainpop.com/
- http://www.kidsworldfun.com/animated_stories_01.php
- http://www.makemegenius.com/
- http://www.turtlediary.com/kids-videos.html

ASSESSMENT

- www.exploratorium.edu/ifi/workshops/assessing/

COMMON CORE STANDARDS

- www.corestandards.org/

GRANTS

- https://www.neafoundation.org/pages/grants-to-educators/
- http://www.annenbergfoundation.org

LANGUAGE ARTS AND SCIENCE

Graphic Organizers

- https://www.eduplace.com/graphicorganizer/
- https://www.eduplace.com/kids/hme/k_5/graphorg/
- http://www.nctm.org/Publications/teaching-children-mathematics/2009/Vol16/Issue4/Mathematical-Graphic-Organizers/

Writing

- http://www.studentreasures.com/teacherslounge/inspiration/writing-activities/science-writing-activities
- https://visualwritingprompts.wordpress.com/category/subjects/science/
- http://www.creative-writing-ideas-and-activities.com/science-writing-prompts.html
- Project CRISS. http://www.projectcriss.com/

MATHEMATICS AND SCIENCE

- Activities that Integrate mathematics and science (AIMS). www.aimsedu.org/
- FOSS Science Education. www.fossweb.com/
- Gizmos. www.explorelearning.com

METHODOLOGY

- BSCS 5E Instructional Model. http://bscs.org/bscs-5e-instructional-model
- *Meaningful science: Teachers doing inquiry + teaching science.* http://www.chem.fsu.edu/~gilmer/PDFs/Meaningful%20sci.pdf

MISCONCEPTIONS

- http://www.nsta.org/elementaryschool/connections/201209AppropriateTopics-ElementaryStudentScienceMisconceptions.pdf
- http://newyorkscienceteacher.com/sci/pages/miscon/subject-index.php

NEXT GENERATION SCIENCE STANDARDS

- http://www.nap.edu/openbook.php?record_id=4962&page=1
- http://www.corestandards.org/
- http://www.nextgenscience.org/sites/ngss/files/Appendix%20M%20Connections%20to%20the%20CCSS%20for%20Literacy_061213.pdf
- Appendix G: Crosscutting concepts. http://www.nextgenscience.org/sites/ngss/files/Appendix%20G%20-%20Crosscutting%20Concepts%20FINAL%20edited%204.10.13.pdf
- Appendix L: Connections to the common core state standards for mathematics. http://www.nextgenscience.org/sites/ngss/files/Appendix-L_CCSS%20Math%20Connections%2006_03_13.pdf
- Appendix M: Connections to the common core state standards for literacy in science and technical subjects. http://www.nextgenscience.org/sites/ngss/files/Appendix%20M%20Connections%20to%20the%20CCSS%20for%20Literacy_061213.pdf

RESOURCES FOR CLASSROOM SUPPLIES

- Carolina Biological Supply. www.carolina.com
- ETA Hand2Mind. www.hand2mind.com
- Explore Learning. www.explorelearning.com
- Frey Scientific. www.freyscientific.com

- Great Source Education Group.
  http://greatsource.info/store/ProductCatalogController?cmd=LP&nextPage
  =GreatSource/gsMainTemplate.jsp?displayMainCell=whoweare.jsp&display
  RightNav=blank
- Learning Resources. www.learningresources.com/
- Nasco. www.enasco.com/science
- National Geographic.
  http://education.nationalgeographic.com/education/?ar_a=1
- Pasco Scientific. www.pasco.com
- Scholastic Teacher. http://www.scholastic.com/home/
- Ward's.
  https://wardsci.com/store/?&WT.term=wards%2520science&WT.source=google
  &WT.campaign=Brand&WT.medium=cpc&WT.srch=1&WT.mc_id=VWR
  _Wards&cshift_ck=2562A148-25EC-4CE8-A951-7BB5D013C1BBcsvk6F
  2L6S&gclid=CjwKEAjwkK6wBRCcoK_tiOT-zFASJAC7RAriUM0AB
  70R2T1jP1JY21R_vG5sMfQZH6azOlwWJauv4xoCq83w_wcB
- http://www.edutopia.org/blog/websites-for-science-teachers-eric-brunsell
- http://www.sciencekids.co.nz/lessonplans.html
- EDU Resource Solutions. http://thefumerogroup.com/Who_We_Are.html

Posters

- http://www.zazzle.com/free+for+teachers+posters
- http://edgalaxy.com/classroom-posters-charts/
- http://www.weareteachers.com/lessons-resources/classroom-printables
- http://busyteacher.org/teaching_ideas_and_techniques/classroom-posters/

RESOURCES FOR CURRICULUM DEVELOPMENT

- http://www.nps.gov/goga/learn/education/outdoor-labs-curriculum.htm
- http://www.nps.gov/teachers/index.htm
- http://www.nps.gov/maca/forteachers/curriculummaterials.htm
- http://school.discoveryeducation.com/sciencefaircentral/?pID=fair

LESSON PLANS

- https://www.discoveryeducation.com/teachers/free-lesson-plans/
- Superkids. www.superkids.com/aweb/pages/reviews/science/
- https://kids.usa.gov/teachers/lesson-plans/science/index.shtml
- http://teachers.net/lessonplans/subjects/science/
- http://www.sharemylesson.com/early-elementary-science-teaching-resources/

INDEX

CPSIA information can be obtained
at www.ICGtesting.com
Printed in the USA
BVOW06s0832250117
474420BV00003B/35/P